Green Light Classrooms

*This book is dedicated to the glowing spark of innovation
burning brightly inside you—the teacher.
Find it, feed it, and watch the flames of creativity grow.
Discover what happens when that fire ignites your teaching,
illuminating it with color, sound, and warmth.
Like the Phoenix, your students will be reborn with
renewed vigor, passion, and enthusiasm for learning.*

Green Light Classrooms

Teaching Techniques That Accelerate Learning

Rich Allen

CORWIN PRESS
A SAGE Company
Thousand Oaks, CA 91320

For information:

Corwin Press
A SAGE Company
2455 Teller Road
Thousand Oaks, California 91320
www.corwinpress.com

SAGE Ltd.
1 Oliver's Yard
55 City Road
London EC1Y 1SP
United Kingdom

SAGE India Pvt. Ltd.
B 1/I 1 Mohan Cooperative
Industrial Area
Mathura Road, New Delhi
India 110 044

SAGE Asia-Pacific Pte. Ltd.
33 Pekin Street #02-01
Far East Square
Singapore 048763

Printed in the United States of America.

Library of Congress Cataloging-in-Publication Data

Allen, Rich (Richard)
Green light classrooms : teaching techniques that accelerate learning / Rich Allen.
    p. cm.
Includes bibliographical references and index.
ISBN 978-1-4129-5609-3 (cloth : acid-free paper)
ISBN 978-1-4129-5610-9 (pbk. : acid-free paper)
    1. Teaching. 2. Effective teaching. 3. Motivation in education. 4. Learning. I. Title.

LB1025.3A435 2008
371.102—dc22   2008020253

This book is printed on acid-free paper.

08   09   10   11   12   10   9   8   7   6   5   4   3   2

Acquisitions Editor:	Cathy Hernandez
Editorial Assistant:	Ena Rosen
Production Editor:	Libby Larson
Copy Editor:	Jennifer Withers
Typesetter:	C&M Digitals (P) Ltd.
Proofreader:	Theresa Kay
Indexer:	Ellen Slavitz
Cover Designer:	Rose Storey
Graphic Designer:	Scott Van Atta

Cartoons on pages 9, 28, 44, 61, 80, 94, 110, 127, 146, and 168 © Education Illustrated, LLC. Used by permission.

Contents

Preface

For more than 25 years I've had the incredibly good fortune to work in a field of educational research sometimes referred to as "brain-based" learning. I've been involved from a variety of angles: from developing one of the very first summer programs for kids based on these emerging concepts in the early 1980s, to earning a PhD in Educational Psychology with a focus on brain research in the mid-1990s, to working directly with teachers for more than a decade on how to actually *apply* these ideas in the classroom. As the field has developed and expanded, I've witnessed some amazing changes in our understanding of what conditions are necessary for effective teaching and learning.

For example, we now know that traditional lecture-based teaching doesn't work for most students. Clear recall depends on students having more than one *type* of memory of a subject. Effective learning requires more than just hearing, reading, or writing about content. As well, teachers need to create additional *layers* of memory by getting students to emotionally engage with the content, or to move, draw, sing, or act it out.

In fact, as the fledging area of brain-based learning research has grown, and the results from studies in diverse areas of brain research and practical observation have started to support and enhance each other, it has become clear that its findings don't relate to one *single* teaching strategy. Instead, we are seeing the rise of critical *themes* for effective teaching—themes that gave rise to this book.

This book is not about one single idea, but about a new philosophy for education, called "Green Light" teaching, which incorporates many *different* teaching techniques. Too often the latest hot idea takes education by storm, and is pushed on teachers at every level to the exclusion and detriment of some excellent teaching strategies. Then, when the driving force behind this latest trend fades, and the idea runs out of steam, it is dropped completely, and the next hot concept leaps into the yawning gap.

For this reason, rather than offering yet another "perfect" way that every classroom MUST be conducted, the Green Light teaching approach outlined in this book simply encourages teachers to move *away* from Red

Light teaching, meaning away from "the way it has always been done." This process of moving away will drive teachers to adopt new approaches, strategies, techniques, concepts, and ideas that will lead to better results at every level of education.

The Green Light strategies outlined in this book offer teachers a starting point for this journey. They model the Green Light philosophy of instruction in a series of research-supported, practical strategies. These strategies will hopefully be useful in themselves, yet perhaps more importantly, they may serve as a jumping off point for teachers to consider other dynamic methods of teaching.

This point begs the question: Why do we need to change our way of teaching? The reason is simultaneously simple and controversial. It is the fact that, despite governments around the world pouring money into education, as stated previously, **traditional lecture-based teaching methods still do not work for the majority of students today**. I believe that, for many people, traditional teaching has never been particularly effective. But especially today, when our students exist in a high-speed, Web-enabled world that gives them intense stimulation and instant gratification, the percentage of students who actually learn in a lecture-based format is now precariously small. This is why we must adopt a new philosophy of teaching that focuses on how to best support our twenty-first-century students in understanding, remembering, and applying educational material.

How This Book Developed

Since the primary objective of this book is to be a practical guide to help teachers develop more effective lessons, in the conceptual stage of manuscript development I asked teachers I have worked with around the world to tell me what strategies were most effective with their students. I asked them to very briefly summarize the old way of teaching the topic (Red Light), how they were now teaching the same topic (Green Light), and the effectiveness of the strategy. That is what you will see in this text: real lessons, written and delivered by real teachers, and the outstanding results their students are really achieving.

These lessons offer clear, concrete examples of how to apply each strategy, how to weave it into lessons, and how to bring it to life in a real and practical way. Rather than providing only a single example of each idea in action, all of the chapters contain a series of demonstration lessons, followed by my own thoughts, reflections, and ideas concerning the best ways of applying the primary Green Light strategy under discussion.

It is worth mentioning that I didn't choose the strategies that define the chapters of this book in advance. Rather, I began by listing some themes that I believed—based on a quarter century's experience in the field—were important in effective teaching. I then prompted the contributors to send me lessons that fit best with these themes, most of them deliberately defined quite vaguely to avoid leading their thinking. As I expected, some of the lessons clearly demonstrated the effectiveness of many of the emerging themes in brain-based teaching. Yet others prompted me to think about different strategies I hadn't previously considered. The strategies included in this book, then, are certainly backed by academic research; however, they are also supported by what can quite accurately be labeled "action research": research done on real kids, in real classes, by real teachers.

As a result, this book has evolved into a compendium of very clear instructional strategies, presented by both demonstration lessons and a discussion of how to apply these ideas in almost any classroom, covering almost any content, with any age student. I encourage readers to explore this book while asking, "That's how *they* applied the strategies, so what does that tell me about how *I* can apply them in my own classroom?" If this thought is uppermost in the reader's mind, the contributing teacher's voices should come through loud and clear. They are speaking directly to you, explaining how a given topic was taught in a Green Light way, sharing the effectiveness of the approach, and in the process offering you ideas on how to mostly effectively teach your own students—so long as you interpret the concepts in the context of your own situation.

Educators Must Act Now!

It's time to rekindle students' enthusiasm for learning. The danger is that traditional, lecture-dominated, Red Light teaching promotes boredom, apathy, and disengagement. This undermines the single most important thing we can teach students today: the critical ability to become a lifelong learner so they can thrive in today's global community.

A Green Light teacher can be someone in any role in education: teacher, teaching assistant, principal, or custodial staff. It can be anyone who is attempting to provide a positive model to students of all ages, the model of someone who, both as a professional and as an individual, is willing to learn, willing to change, and willing to seek ways to improve life in all its various dimensions. The goal of this book is to inspire such educators to become experimenters, explorers, and researchers in their own right, every day in their classrooms. This will create an ever-expanding universe of teaching strategies to replace the Red Light teaching practices that no longer work in today's classrooms.

I believe that each educator will, over time, develop his or her unique style of teaching. I not only encourage this endeavor, I applaud it loudly and support it with all my heart. If the strategies suggested in this book are useful in guiding teachers toward this type of ongoing professional development, then the book will have been successful at its most fundamental level.

I hope that, by describing in detail what is being done in some schools, by some very courageous teachers, this book offers educators, faculty, and staff two vital elements to empower Green Light teaching:

1. *the confidence* that these alternative teaching strategies really work; and

2. the *knowledge* of exactly *how* to use the strategies to improve educational outcomes.

In my experience, once teachers are empowered in this way, they and their students achieve truly outstanding results.

Acknowledgments

The backbone of this book is the wonderful lessons that have been so generously offered by the contributing teachers. The author wishes to personally thank these pioneering individuals for giving so freely of their innovative, imaginative, and inspired ideas, so their educational colleagues throughout the world may ultimately benefit:

Marcia Beldock	Wayne Logue
Tina Bernard	Kris Long
Kim Cooke	Eva Matz
Jenn Currie	Greg Rayer
Sheryl Fainges	Tiffany Reindl
Peggy Frum	Karen Renaud
Karoline Gebbett	Cindy Rickert
Keil Hileman	Shari Rindels
Sarah Hofstra	Christy Sheffield
Rob Jensen	Katie Sloan
Emma Jeter	Kristine Sobbe
Paul Jungel	Mary Storrs
Duke Kelly	Therese Vitiello

In addition, the author wishes to individually thank three special people for their specific contributions to the manuscript.

- **Karen Pryor**, an astonishingly talented editor, who took my original words and helped bring them to vivid, vibrant life. Her efforts have provided a friendly voice and conversational tone to every aspect of this manuscript, making it a far more readable, understandable, and ultimately *useful* book than I could have ever hoped to produce on my own. You are amazing at what you do.

- **Wayne Logue**, a gifted and insightful professional cartoonist, for providing the wonderful illustrations included throughout the manuscript.
- **Kim Rundhaug**, for her excellent research efforts.

To everyone listed here, thank you so much for bringing this work to life. Without each of you, it would not exist. With you, together, hopefully we have created a motivating and moving resource other educators will look to for encouragement as they continue their own professional journey, and develop their own Green Light lessons.

PUBLISHER'S ACKNOWLEDGMENTS

Corwin Press gratefully acknowledges the contributions of the following reviewers:

Jacie Bejster
First-Grade Teacher, Fort Pitt Elementary School
Pittsburgh, PA

Jason Cushner
Math Teacher, Eagle Rock School and
Professional Development Center
Boulder, CO

Michelle Drechsler
Language Arts Teacher, Sonoran Trails Middle School
Phoenix, AZ

Renee Peoples
Fourth-Grade Teacher, Swain West Elementary
Bryson City, NC

Daniel Rubenstein
Math Teacher, Collegiate School
New York, NY

Leon Strecker
Technology Teacher, Darien High School
Darien, CT

Beth Wile
Science Teacher, Union Park Middle School
Orlando, FL

Amy Woods
Humanities Teacher, Nashua High School North
Manchester, NH

About the Author

Richard Allen, PhD, is a highly regarded educator and master trainer with more than 25 years' experience coaching teachers. Founder and President of Green Light Education, he has taken his "Impact Teaching" strategies beyond the United States and Canada to such diverse locations as the United Kingdom, Australia, New Zealand, Hong Kong, Singapore, Brunei, Russia, Jordan, and Brazil. Dr. Allen is also a popular keynote speaker at international education conferences and works with schools and school districts to embed effective teaching methods into mainstream curriculum.

Dr. Allen first took to the stage as an off-Broadway actor, before starting his educational career as a high school math and drama teacher. In 1985 he became a lead facilitator for SuperCamp—an accelerated learning program for teens—and has since worked with more than 25,000 students worldwide. Dr. Allen completed his doctorate in Educational Psychology at Arizona State University, where he studied how the human brain receives, processes, and recalls information—knowledge that informs all aspects of his teaching strategies. The author resides in the U.S. Virgin Islands on the sun-kissed paradise of St. Croix and can be reached at his e-mail address: rich@drrichallen.com.

1 Overview

Green means . . . go!

RED VERSUS GREEN: WHAT'S THE DIFFERENCE?

Imagine the scene. It's 8:00 a.m. and the beginning of a typical high-school history class. As usual, students are instructed to open their books to a certain page and get ready to take notes. After a few minutes, where the teacher struggles to keep discipline, most students have their books open at the proper place, and the teacher begins to talk about the Second World War. For an hour, a group of yawning, disinterested students wish they were somewhere else. The conscientious grudgingly take notes; others stare out of the window. When class ends, few—if any—of the students will recall much of the material from the lesson.

Welcome to "Red Light" teaching: the traditional, lecture-saturated educational approach that STOPS students from learning—an approach that dampens students' enthusiasm for education and makes some actually dread going to school. Sadly, in the majority of our schools, this is how learning is being presented to many young minds (Jensen, 2005).

This book contends it doesn't have to be this way and offers teachers an alternative approach, currently being pioneered all over the world, identified by this book as "Green Light" teaching. Green Light teachers are armed with a host of new strategies that re-START, empower, and ignite the learning process. In a Green Light classroom, students are excited about learning; cognition and recall improves dramatically; and teachers have far fewer discipline issues. In a Green Light school, students look forward to lessons; learning takes place in an atmosphere of laughter and excitement; and every class exceeds its testing targets.

Importantly, because Green Light teaching incorporates emotions, drama, art, and music, students who learn in a Green Light classroom don't just master lessons; they also discover and expand their creativity. In an age where employers want people who "can think intuitively, who are imaginative and innovative, who can communicate well" (Robinson, 2001), developing students' creativity may be just as important as teaching academic skills.

Is this just wishful thinking, a hopeful delusion? No—this is REAL! As this book proves, courageous teachers from all over the world are already using Green Light teaching—and getting astonishing results. They are proving every day, over and over, that *every* student can achieve outstanding results . . . if they are taught properly!

RED LIGHT TEACHERS

Here's a real life example of a Red Light teacher (who, for obvious reasons, will remain anonymous). This particular Red Light teacher has been teaching high school for more than two decades and would describe himself as a very good teacher. He knows his content; he has organized his lessons and prepared his worksheets. But his lesson plans incorporate only ONE

Figure 1.1 Red Light Teaching, Green Light Teaching

Red Light Teaching	Green Light Teaching
Traditional, one-way teaching strategies	Unconventional, interactive strategies
Students are expected to sit quietly and only listen to the teacher	Students are involved in the learning process
Learning occurs through listening, repeating, reading, and writing	Learning occurs through listening, repeating, reading, writing, moving, drawing, singing, social interaction, emotional engagement, creativity, novelty, pictures, and drama
Students are often bored, undisciplined, and unmotivated	Students are engaged, attentive, and self-motivated and take responsibility for their own learning
Lessons are tailored to and dictated by the subject matter	Lessons are tailored to the students and dictated by their interests and priorities

mode of instruction (lecturing), ONE cognition strategy (completing work-sheets), and ONE assessment method (written tests).

He doesn't take into account the needs of the majority of kids in his classroom who find it hard to learn from just listening, reading, and writing. He gives no thought to visual or kinesthetic learners. He doesn't use music or novelty to engage reluctant learners and encode strong memories. He doesn't embed cognition through drama, drawing, or social interaction. He doesn't adapt his content to what is current, significant, or of interest to his students (Tate, 2002), and he doesn't teach them how to *remember* that content.

He believes that if he says it, they will know it. From his point of view, how well they do on the test is entirely up to them: they can choose either to learn the material or not. It has never occurred to him that many of his students don't know *how* to learn effectively. He thinks the bell curve tests results he gets each year reflect his students' inability to learn—not his inability to teach.

Red Light teachers like this often speak with the certainty of ignorance. They know it all, because they've been there, they've been around, and they've learned all they'll ever need to know about teaching. But these teachers are frequently using strategies that are 20, 30, or even 100 years old! Perhaps these strategies were once entirely appropriate teaching techniques; perhaps they weren't. Regardless, they are no longer fit for use in today's classrooms, with today's students (Willis, 2005).

Most teachers recognize the truth of this, at least subconsciously. Recently, this author witnessed a school attempting to initiate some faculty development. To improve understanding of a typical student's experience of school, teachers were asked to "shadow" students for an entire day. The teachers rebelled, saying they didn't want to "sit through all those 'boring' classes." WHAT? Shouldn't this be a sign that things must change? If teachers themselves think the classes are too boring to sit through, what must the students think?

GREEN LIGHT TEACHERS

By stark contrast, Green Light teachers realize that how *they* learned at school—sitting still and listening to the teacher—didn't really work for them and certainly isn't working with today's students. Instead, they adjust their strategies to match the fast, exciting, interactive world their students live in (Sousa, 2002).

Following the simple, yet revolutionary, belief that outstanding results are truly possible for *every* student, Green Light teachers choose from a range of dynamic new teaching strategies and consciously plan lessons based on what engages their students and suits their learning styles. In this approach, seven year olds pick up French vocabulary in a drawing game; teenagers make up and perform rap songs to remember facts about ocean strata; kids turn their own hands into a map of Alaska; and nine year olds "jump" spelling words on a life-size alphabet grid.

Green Light teachers get astonishing results—and not just in terms of getting *every* kid to pass the test. They also turn reluctant learners into excited students who go home and enthuse to their amazed parents about the cool things they learned at school. They give shy, barely articulate English students the confidence to chatter with fluency in a second language. They allow high school students to rediscover the enthusiasm for learning they came into the world with (Schiefele, 1991).

Green Light teachers know that students only learn if they enjoy their education and are completely involved in it, so these teachers make learning fun and empower students to create their own learning strategies and succeed (Robinson, 2001). In fact, the overarching objective of every Green Light teacher is to give their students as many chances as possible, every day, in every way, to *realize and celebrate their own brilliance.*

In a Green Light classroom, *every* child can achieve outstanding results; students who fail in Red Light classrooms can discover the value and excitement of being a successful learner. For these students in particular, Green Light teaching is a beacon of hope. Showing them they can learn almost anything restores their sense of self-worth and gives them confidence in their ability to achieve. Little wonder Green Light teachers rarely have discipline issues.

GREEN LIGHT STRATEGIES: THE FOUNDATION

Before we examine the nine strategies presented in this book, a note of clarification is needed:

> These are not the <u>only</u> ideas teachers could use to move away from Red Light teaching—there are <u>many</u> more.

The following strategies were simply chosen to give teachers a manageable foundation from which to begin designing and delivering lessons that align with the Green Light philosophy. They are as follows:

- **Memory**   Pegs, association, body location, acrostics, and rhyming
- **Connections**   Creating meaning; allowing students to own the material

- **Movement**   Physically engaging students in the learning process
- **Novelty**   Harnessing something *different* to capture students' attention
- **Tone**   Music, chants, and teacher's tonal changes and pauses
- **Emotion**   Using laughter and surprise to fire curiosity and excitement
- **Socialization** Student-to-student discussions, processing, and debriefs
- **Drama**   Theatrics, storytelling, and students' acting the learning out
- **Visuals**   Posters, mind maps, doodles, and drawing

You may ask, "But where did these strategies come from? Did they come from academic research? Are they pulled from theoretical papers?" No. In fact, although they are backed up by educational and psychological research, they are based on *action-research* evidence. Over 200 Green Light teachers were originally consulted in writing this book. As they sent in sample lessons describing what they considered to be Green Light teaching, these nine strategies emerged consistently across every age range and discipline.

The point is: this is not just theory; this is real. The lessons that illustrate the following chapters are drawn from actual classroom experiences. Students throughout the world are benefiting from these techniques every day—just as, tomorrow, yours could too.

How to Use the Strategies

Like any type of teaching, the starting place for Green Light instruction is the topic. However, notice how, as shown by its position in the yellow circle of the stoplight diagram (see Figure 1.2 on page 6), we must approach our topic with caution. In this case, the caution is because, as we start to plan a lesson, we must consider two issues: not just the topic, but also our students. In Green Light teaching, we design every lesson so it best offers the *students* the chance of understanding and remembering it.

To achieve this, rather than remaining static in the Red Light circle with the same, repetitive strategies, we need to instead move down into the Green Light circle, where there are a multitude of possible strategies to engage students in the lesson. The rays bursting out of the Green Light circle remind us to ask ourselves: Could there be any chance for movement, for the use of music, for a specific memory strategy? Has a relevant connection been created, and if not, is it an important issue to address given the nature of this topic? The answers to questions like these will help us design more dynamic and effective lessons.

Figure 1.2   Red Light Teaching STOPS the Learning Process

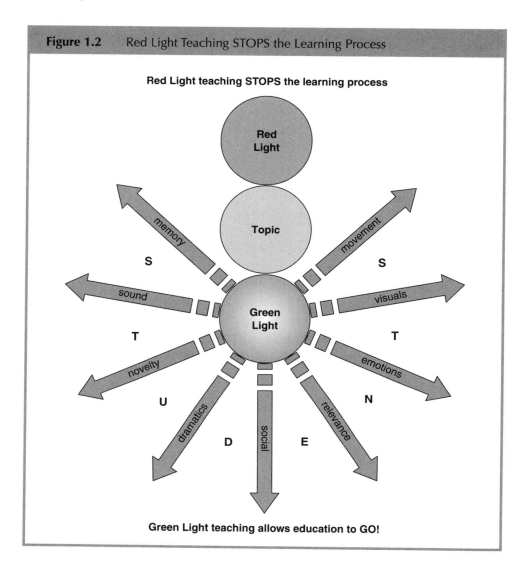

Here are some other important ideas to bear in mind when using the strategies:

Select With Care

Green Light teaching is *not* about using all the strategies in every lesson we present. Don't try to force them into your lesson plan. That said, it's very difficult to use only one of these concepts in isolation, because employing one seems to naturally open the door to another. So don't be surprised if you find yourself weaving many of the concepts together, like threads in an educational tapestry. It doesn't matter whether you use one thread or all of them. If your lesson works—if your students enjoy, recall, and apply it—then you chose correctly.

Every Learning Situation Is Different

For every lesson, Green Light teachers consider how best to get the material across to *this* group of students, on *this* day, at *this* time. A strategy that works in the morning might not fit in the afternoon. One that is effective on a Monday might not generate the same level of student interest on a Friday. Another that works with one group of students might not fit at all for another group. This doesn't necessarily mean that we have to throw away a previously successful lesson plan. It just means that we must be aware when students lose focus, and have a host of strategies in our repertoire to re-energize the group and find new ways for them to connect with the material.

It's Not Just Entertainment

A Red Light teacher recently stated, "I'm not here to entertain the students!" However, upon hearing those words, a Green Light teacher responded with an important distinction, saying, "True, I'm not here to entertain either. However, I am here to *engage,* and sometimes engagement requires entertainment." That wonderful line sums up much of the intention of these strategies. While students may indeed be much more *entertained* in a Green Light classroom, this is merely a positive side effect. If students are entertained and engaged, they will apply themselves more fully to the learning process. In other words, entertaining teaching results in higher levels of engagement—opening the door to higher levels of learning.

There Are No Absolutes

For all its benefits, Green Light teaching is not the single best way to teach all material. Lessons are never completely one or the other, simply green or red. There are usually opportunities to weave "shades of green" into many aspects of teaching. For example, there will certainly be times where lecture—by itself a Red Light approach—may in fact be the most efficient method of delivering a limited amount of content. In this situation, merely providing students a hint of green—perhaps by occasionally allowing them to talk with other students to process the information—may be enough. At the opposite end of the spectrum, it is also certainly true that not all lessons should be BRIGHT GREEN—meaning wild, radical, unique, and bizarre. Sometimes a simple twist in the lesson—a shading of green—may suffice.

Green Light Teaching Is Easier on Teachers

Red Light teachers often imagine that traditional instruction is easier than using Green Light strategies. However, this is an illusion. Since students are frequently bored, Red Light teachers often encounter higher levels of disciplinary issues. Moreover, because many students in a Red Light classroom don't learn the necessary material, subject matter needs to be reviewed again and again. Perhaps most importantly, in teaching the same old way, year after year, Red Light teachers themselves can become bored or burnt out— some even dread coming to school themselves. Red Light teaching is definitely the lazy way to approach teaching, but in the long run it is not easy.

Green Light Teaching Works for Students of All Ages

Because some Green Light strategies, such as movement or music, are already used quite commonly by early primary teachers, it's easy to fall into the trap of imagining that these techniques are only appropriate for younger students. Not so! All of these strategies—appropriately adapted for the sophistication of the students—are relevant for learners of any age. In fact, it could be argued that, as older students lose their innate enthusiasm for learning and become cynical and disillusioned about education, they need Green Light strategies more than ever.

No One Wants to Be a Red Light Teacher!

Few teachers head eagerly for school in the anticipation that today will be the day they totally bore their students to death! Most teachers would much rather use strategies that ignite students' interest in the classroom. The problem is that many teachers aren't aware of Green Light techniques, and even those who are don't feel they have "permission" to use them, because they're not "mainstream." One of the objectives of this book is to address both of those issues. The more teachers who embrace Green Light teaching—who dare to be different and creative—the more other teachers will become aware there is an alternative, and the more acceptable Green Light teaching will become. So don't keep the strategies in this book to yourself. If you find something that works, share it with your colleagues. Don't just be a Green Light classroom; be a Green Light school!

Hope for the Future of Education

Red Light classrooms are frequently caricatured hilariously in movies such as *Ferris Bueller's Day Off* or *Fast Times at Ridgemont High*. Yet, as audiences laugh at these over-the-top depictions of a boring classroom, there is often an undercurrent of discomfort in the laughter at the scenes of failed education. This is because many of us have been there and experienced the reality of those moments ourselves—and we know that little may have changed.

Why is it, as we "move past" school, that many adults choose to forget, or deem as inevitable, the learning experiences we did *not* enjoy? If they didn't work for us, why do we imagine that those archaic learning styles are appropriate for the dynamic, hyperspace-invading current generation?

Why, when there is overwhelming evidence that we are not reaching our students in the ways needed to help them become involved, contributing members of society, do we continue to do the same things we've always done, over and over and over?

As teachers, we should be laughing happily at those movies, safe in the knowledge that the education system they portray is no longer real. We should be able to say, "Thank goodness that's not the way things are in the classroom anymore!" But we can't, because that's exactly the way it is in the majority of classrooms.

Yet there is always hope. As Green Light teachers, we have the opportunity to change the way we teach the next generation. We can use Green Light strategies to create dynamic learning environments for both students *and* teachers. We can draw learners in with excitement and enthusiasm. We can make our schools places students can't wait to get to and are sad to leave behind.

And we don't even have to blaze the trail. The teachers whose lessons illustrate this book are already doing it—and in the process they are illuminating the lives of thousands of students. All we have to do is open our minds to the possibilities of Green Light teaching and dare to follow them. If we are to truly believe that *every* student can achieve outstanding results, then we need to actively seek out the strategies and techniques—both large and small—that can make this axiom the literal, everyday truth in every classroom.

2 Memory

If they can't remember it, they never learned it.

Does this happen in your classroom? Students start the year confident because the first things they learn are intriguing and easy ways to memorize information. They arrive to each class enthusiastic about applying these strategies. Actual classroom time is devoted to adapting the memorization strategies to fit the day's lesson content. In tests, students are excited by the amount and depth of information they can easily recall.

MEMORY: AN OVERVIEW

Students are rarely—if ever—actually taught how to encode and attach recall prompts to the information they need to learn. Instead, they are given the command "Learn it" without any actual instruction on *how* that process—learning, encoding, and then recalling—actually occurs. But this presumes that students somehow (perhaps magically?) know how their memory works, how information is encoded along different memory paths—audio, visual, kinesthetic, emotional, and so forth—and how to create recall prompts that trigger the process of retrieving the information.

Interestingly, while it's acceptable to use a few simple recall prompts, such as acrostics, with younger students, this practice diminishes as students get older. Red Light teachers seem to believe learning becomes a "listen and get it" situation and memory strategies are no longer appropriate once students get to about 10 years old. If you ask Red Light teachers about using recall prompts with older students, they will typically say, "Oh, those things are for little children—not for young adults!" How wrong they are! The truth is, outside those rare individuals with so-called photographic—eidetic—memories, *everyone* needs recall prompts and multiple memory encodings to remember new information effectively.

By ignoring this simple fact, Red Light teaching has perpetuated one of the greatest injustices of our education systems. In Red Light teaching, students who *stumble* across good memory strategies make great leaps forward in education, while equally adept students who do not stumble across these techniques often decide, because they find recall difficult, that they aren't "smart enough" and begin a downward spiral in their learning process.

The operative word here is *stumble*! Red Light teaching leaves students to figure out memory strategies for themselves. It places successful learning in the hands of chance. How dare we do that to our children? How can we allow students to think they're "dumb" when they simply lack the knowledge of how to remember information? It seems outrageous to leave them to fend for themselves—to sink or swim without our help—in this crucial aspect of learning.

One of the most profound philosophical differences between Red Light and Green Light instruction is that Green Light teachers do *not* leave learning to chance. Instead, they directly *show* students how to remember new information. They tell their students explicitly *why* they remember certain things and forget others; then they show them *how* to apply these ideas to their own learning process. They deliberately design lesson plans that will encode information along redundant retrieval routes—in multiple memory pathways—and build in, or teach their students to create their own, recall prompts. In doing so, they lay the foundations for lifelong learning—by empowering students to remember any information they want to.

This process is twofold: First, Green Light teachers *model* recall strategies in their lessons; and second, they make them *explicit* so students can learn how to apply the ideas themselves. As with so much in education, everything starts with the model. If students can see the ideas applied, repeatedly, they will see it as a natural step to apply these ideas elsewhere in their schoolwork—and, perhaps more important, in their lives.

While this chapter provides many examples of lessons that both model and teach memory strategies, it does not cover the theory of memory, nor does it thoroughly teach specific memory techniques. Teachers wishing to learn more about either of these topics will find a suggested reading list at the end of this chapter.

Instead, this chapter is intended to show teachers how easy it is to give students the sense of success they can achieve through using and applying simple, practical memory strategies. These strategies will prove to students that they *are* smart and they *can* learn anything if it is taught to them properly. If students experience frequent success, they will develop the inner drive to succeed in both school and life. All kids have the right to know that they are smart. By teaching them in a way that focuses on *how* they will remember the information, Green Light teachers can lead them to this vital conclusion about themselves. This may seem like a lofty goal, yet note how easily it is accomplished in this first lesson.

LESSON 1

Memorizing information through acronyms, acrostics, and association

Topic	Alaskan Geography
Students	Fourth Grade: ages 9–10
Primary Green Light strategy	Memory
Related strategies	Novelty, connections, and movement
Submitted by	Mary Storrs, Fourth-Grade Teacher
	Sherrod Elementary
	Palmer, Alaska

Red Light. Traditionally, a teacher would hand the kids a copy of the state map, point to the region, and say its name. The students would repeat, color, or maybe tell a friend what region is there. Each region would get a new color. The evening's homework? You guessed it. Study the map and remember where each region is located. Tomorrow we'll have the test!

Green Light. We memorize the regions of Alaska using the back of our right hand as a map, verbal cues, and oral cast make the map. To do this, make a "gun" with your first finger and thumb, bend your fingers at the first knuckle, and keep them flat at the second knuckle. Turn your hand over and rotate so the index finger is pointing southwest. Ta-dah: This becomes our "handy"-dandy Alaska map! (See Figure 2.1.)

There are six regions. The students and I came up with ideas to remember each area:

- For the Panhandle/Southeast, we say (and do) "grab the Southeast 'pan' handle" (thumb).
- South Central is the soft part between the thumb and index finger. We say "squishy squishy South Central" and squish the soft part. We live in this region and the kids get a kick out of living in "squishy squishy South Central"!
- Interior is inside, so we "tickle" the back of the hand and say "tickle the interior."
- The North Slope is at the top of the hand (along the bent pinky and side). Since it is snowy, we "slide on the slope" (slide our finger along the area).
- Bering Sea/West Coast is the four bent fingers. We tap one knuckle for each word, "Bering Sea/West Coast."
- For the Alaska Peninsula and Aleutian Chain, we run our finger along the index finger and say "Alaska Peninsula" and then tap our finger to represent the string of islands while we say "Aleutian Chain."

Every time we need a map of Alaska, we just "take out our handy dandy Alaska map."

Effectiveness. Before we came up with this memorization tool, the kids did very poorly on the tests and future references to the locations of the areas. After, they ALL scored 100 percent and have no problem remembering what area is where—even later in the year.

DEBRIEF OF LESSON 1

In this lesson, the students are learning by *associating* something that is familiar with something that is new. Association is the idea of connecting two things together, where seeing—or remembering—one thing triggers the memory of the other. It means relating something we want to learn to something we already know. Teachers can apply this idea in countless ways, such as having students connect key concepts to objects around the room, or giving out an object that is mentally tied to a subject—so seeing it again will bring back classroom discussions about that topic.

Figure 2.1   Alaska Map

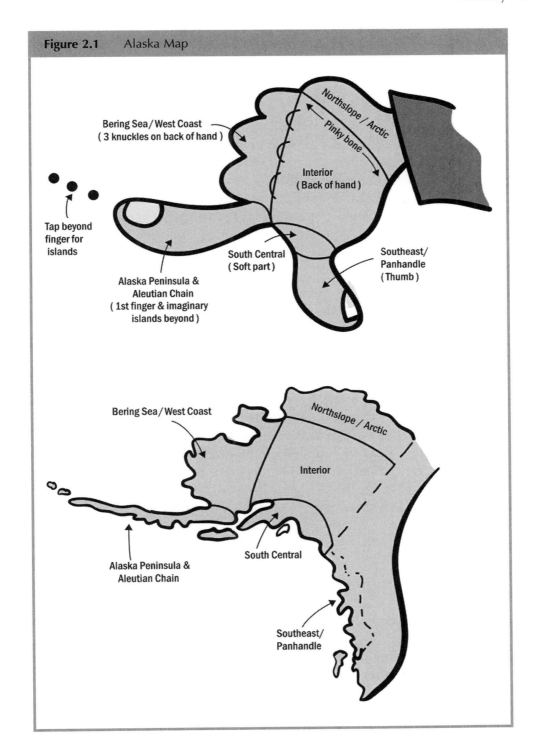

On a very broad level, association is in action whenever you hear someone say, "That reminds me . . ." You've probably experienced it when someone asked you to do something for them and then, having said yes, you completely forgot until you saw them again. Seeing them triggered the memory of what you were supposed to have done. You probably said, "Oh, I'm so sorry, I forgot!" Actually, the truth is that you didn't forget, you just remembered, at an inconvenient time! What you needed was a trigger that would help your memory fire at the right time.

Green Light teachers use as many association triggers as possible. For example, acronyms and acrostics are two simple memory strategies that function similarly to association and can be applied to a wide variety of topics.

Acronyms

An acronym is a word made out of the first letters of the items to be remembered. For example, the word HOMES is often used to teach students the five Great Lakes. Using this device, can you name them? (Huron, Ontario, Michigan, Erie, and Superior.) Do you know what SCUBA actually stands for? In fact, did you even know it *was* an acronym? (Self-Contained Underwater Breathing Apparatus.) Similarly, ROY G. BIV represents the colors of the spectrum, in order! Given this memory device, could you guess what they are? (Red, Orange, Yellow, Green, Blue, Indigo, and Violet.)

Acronyms "chunk" information so students don't have to remember a lot of information all at once. Of course, an acronym is not the original information, only a cue to help you retrieve the information. However, it's useful because it changes a recall task to an *aided* recall task and also provides information on how *many* items need to be recalled (ROY G. BIV = seven colors).

Acrostics

An acrostic is a series of words in which the first letters form a useful word or phrase. For example, an acrostic to remember the Great Lakes might be Healthy Old Men Eat Slowly. One well-known acrostic from music class is Every Good Boy Does Fine—representing the notes on the lines of the treble clef. Another one from math class is Please Excuse My Dear Aunt Sally, representing the order of operations to be done in a math problem (Parentheses, Exponents, Multiplication, Division, Addition, and Subtraction). For more on teaching this particular lesson, see the chapter on social interaction.

Acrostics, much like acronyms, may be more useful to students if the material is somewhat familiar. Since it provides only a trigger, students will still need to generate the original information. This means we also need to help them connect the acrostic *to the right material* in some way, such as saying, "Every good boy does fine, when playing the piano."

But simple acronyms and acrostics are just the start. As this next lesson shows, we can use a story as a mnemonic device to help students remember more complex information.

LESSON 2

Memorizing information through storytelling techniques

Topic	Weather—Layers of the Atmosphere
Students	Sixth Grade: ages 11–12
Primary Green Light strategy	Memory
Related strategies	Drama, movement, and connections
Submitted by	Tiffany Reindl, Fifth-and Sixth-Grade Teacher
	Jefferson School for the Arts
	Stevens Point, Wisconsin

Red Light. Traditionally, this topic is introduced in the text of a science book followed by a worksheet asking the students to label a diagram of the layers of the atmosphere.

Green Light. Before my students could learn the more advanced information about weather, they needed to have a good grasp of where weather takes place and the basic vocabulary of the layers of the atmosphere. Since we had already used acronyms for other vocabulary, I decided to write a short story for them to learn. On Monday when they arrived, they were greeted by the following story on an overhead.

Trop and Strat

There was once a really **cool** foot doctor named **Trop**. He had **3.6 degrees** from **1,000 feet** universities. He was smart but usually felt under the **weather**—until he fell in love with a girl named **Strat**. She was really **hot**, although she tended to **zone** out when he talked. After dating awhile, Trop asked Strat if she wanted to "**Meso**round." Strat gave him the **cold** shoulder and told him to go turn up the **therm**ostat if he needed to **warm** up. She was going dancing **at The Sphere**.

The students react to this love story with giggles as I read it out loud to them. I tell them that this story is going to be very important to them but I'm not going to tell them how. I challenge them to see if they can figure it out. Their homework is to tell it to several people and see if anyone knows why they are learning it. I repeat the story again over several days, leaving out key phrases for them to fill in. I have them tell it to someone sitting near them, and their audience can only help by actions if they get stuck.

One day, a huge inflatable microphone turns a class into a comedy club as I invite students who think they have it memorized to come up and perform it. Even the students who aren't bold enough to perform are waiting for the slightest hesitation so they can call out assistance from the peanut gallery.

Finally, usually several days later, in our reading someone comes across one of the terms and makes the connection to the story. In our science text, the information is in the form of an illustration. The students eagerly point out to each other the connections between the picture and the story:

> See, Trop is the really the first layer of the atmosphere, called the *troposphere*. As you go up in altitude, the temperature becomes cooler by 3.6 degrees Fahrenheit for every 1,000 feet. It is in this layer that weather occurs. The second layer is the *stratosphere*, indicated by an increase in temperature. This is the layer where ozone is found. The third layer, the *mesosphere*, where the temperature becomes cooler again, is followed by the *thermosphere*, which increases in temperature as you go up in altitude. Together, all of these layers form the *atmosphere* (at-the-sphere).

This last line usually gets the biggest groan, followed by accusations of being corny, but they love it—and they learn the information!

Effectiveness. For information to be retained by students, it must connect to what they already know, be presented in a novel way that captures their interest, and be reviewed over a length of time. Add in fun and a situation full of anticipation, and you can easily see how this story is unforgettable. Now, whenever I have a few extra minutes, I just begin the first sentence and listen to my students fill in the rest.

DEBRIEF OF LESSON 2

For a variety of reasons, stories seem to be easy for many people to recall (Alna, 1999). In the case of this lesson, the story became a mnemonic device (also occasionally referred to as the "linking" strategy) in which the teacher wove the items students need to recall. The use of stories in the classroom is important because it can serve multiple functions simultaneously, such as acting as a memory device while also increasing other critical skills, such as literacy (Brand, 2006).

Formulas, processes that have distinct steps, and specific lists all lend themselves easily to this storytelling memory aid. Simply take a series of concepts, terms, or ideas like these and link them in a continuous, integrated sequence that creates a chain of associations. Try to build as much visual imagery into the story as possible, because this will make it even easier for your students to remember.

However, teachers don't always have to be the ones doing the work! When students make up their own stories, the process of forming the story and the ownership this creates makes the information even more memorable. Try asking students to form small groups and create their own stories, which can be shared aloud. Then you have a choice: students can either keep their own story to practice or decide as a class which story would be the easiest to help them remember the information. Either way works fine.

One example of the storytelling method in action took place several years ago at a high school in Phoenix. The author had introduced this idea to teachers at a workshop, and they took it back to their classrooms. Several months later, a teacher sent an e-mail, sharing a story the students had made up to help them remember the quadratic equation. The equation is

$$x = \frac{-b \pm \sqrt{b^2 - 4ac}}{2a}$$

The story they made up was as follows:

There was a very *negative* boy (–b). He was *undecided* (±) about going to a *radical* party (*radical symbol*). He was such a square boy (b²) that he *lost out* (–) on 4 awesome chicks! (4ac). The party was *over* by 2am (2a).

The students thought this was extremely funny, but it helped them remember the equation, and do well on the test for that topic.

The specific memorization strategies mentioned so far can all be applied many ways in the course of teaching a lesson. Each has its place and time. The next lesson, however, outlines a strategy that combines several of these ideas into one concept. It may be the single most flexible, adaptable, and powerful strategy that teachers can share with their students. Once students learn it and fully understand how to apply it, many will remember and utilize it for the rest of their lives.

LESSON 3

Memorizing information through the pegging method

Topic	Ocean Facts
Students	Fifth Grade: ages 10–11
Primary Green Light strategy	Memory

Related strategies	Movement, emotion, and connections
Submitted by	Emma Jeter, Fifth-Grade Teacher
	Christopher Farms Elementary School
	Virginia Beach, Virginia

Red Light. Traditionally, students are lectured to about the ocean and are given a worksheet to fill out.

Green Light. First, I teach my students a memory strategy call "pegging." In this strategy, they are taught to connect the numbers 1 through 20 to a specific item, using hand motions each time. Here is the list of "pegs" I teach them:

The Peg	The Action
1. Sun	Make a circle with your hands.
2. Eyes	Bring two fingers to your eyes.
3. Triangle	Draw a triangle in the air with your fingers.
4. Stove	Touch all four burners on a stove.
5. Fingers	Hold up the five fingers of one hand.
6. Sticks	Pick up sticks from the ground.
7. 7UP	Take a big drink from a can of 7UP.
8. Octopus	Put your arms out like an octopus.
9. Line	Draw a line in the air in front of you.
10. Hen	Flap your arms like a hen's wings.
11. Fence	Hold two fingers in the air, and make a series of fence posts.
12. Eggs	Crack an imaginary egg.
13. Black cat	Pet the cat.
14. Heart	Make a heart in the air in front of you with your fingers.
15. Fame	Arms spread wide, say "Fame!"
16. Driving	Drive an imaginary car.
17. Magazine	Turn the pages of an imaginary magazine.
18. Vote	Make a check mark in the air.
19. TV remote	Click the imaginary remote at the TV.
20. 20–20 vision	Make circles with your hands around your eyes.

They learn these pegs and then practice them many times. While I use them in different ways throughout the year, here's how I use them in the ocean zones lesson. We connect (associate) the pegs to the 20 most important facts I want them to know. Those facts are as follows:

Twenty Facts About the Ocean: A Peg List

1. The ocean covers 70 percent of the earth's surface. (Think of the sun as a big O for oceans.)

2. A current is a river of water running through the ocean. (Make a current with your two fingers.)

3. An ocean trench is the deepest area of the ocean floor. (Make an upside-down triangle—the shape of a trench.)

4. The abyssal plain is the level area of the ocean floor. (Smooth out the floor with your stove top.)

5. Phytoplankton float on the surface of the ocean, producing oxygen. (Make your five fingers touch the surface of the ocean.)

6. Benthic organisms live on the bottom of the ocean. (Reach down and pick up a benthic organism.)

7. Nekton are marine organisms that can swim or move against the current. (Imagine you are reaching up to the surface of the ocean.)

8. The Gulf Stream is an ocean current that affects our climate. (Make the octopus swim in the Gulf Stream.)

9. The feature of the ocean floor near the shore that dives down is called the continental slope. (Draw the line going down the continental slope.)

10. The continental shelf links the shoreline to the continental slope. (Make a shelf with your hen wings.)

11. The continental rise is a collection of sand and sediment at the bottom of the continental slope. (Make your fence posts rise.)

12. The mid-ocean ridge is a mountain range along the ocean floor. (Make your egg into the shape of the ocean ridge.)

13. Waves are caused by wind, and water moves in circles. (Stroke the cat and make waves.)

14. Tides are caused by the gravitational pull of the moon. (Make your heart start at the moon and end at the ocean.)

15. Salinity is the amount of salt in the ocean water. (Put salt shakers in your hands and sprinkle salt.)

16. Zooplankton are microscopic organisms that cannot swim against the current. (Imagine driving and not getting anywhere.)

17. An ecosystem is the whole ocean environment and the organisms in it. (Open your magazine and see the whole ocean.)

18. Another word for the ocean floor is ocean basin. (Make two vote check marks to remind you of two words meaning the same thing.)

19. Freshwater has low salinity. (Use your remote to change the volume or salinity of water.)

20. I can see how smart I am! (A celebration!)

Effectiveness. It's amazing! Once they have pegged these basic facts, they can usually remember right away all the things that we talked about concerning each fact. The memory peg acts as a trigger to bring back to mind everything else that we discussed about that fact. Tests on the ocean zones are a cinch, because the students simply make the motion with their hands, which triggers the associated fact about the ocean, and they know the answers!

DEBRIEF OF LESSON 3

The subject students are learning about in this lesson is ocean facts, but we can apply the peg system of remembering to any subject. The key is to ensure that our students know the pegs first. Those pegs stay the same in any situation; what changes is the subject matter. Green Light teachers are using pegs to help students remember a Shakespearean monologue, by pegging the first word of each line, and facts from ancient history. One teenager even memorized the 14 steps of her equestrian routine this way!

For younger students who don't have the life experience to understand the connections of the 20 original pegs, we can use *body location* pegs instead. This is similar to the original pegs, except that instead of connecting the numbers to an object, young students learn 10 positions on their body. This memory method starts by teaching students locations on their body connected to different numbers. Once this connection has been established, students "locate" material—make connections—to these locations. While this works for students of all ages, it is primarily used with younger children. One example might be to teach the eight planets of the solar system using this method. Here are 10 basic locations on the body you would teach first:

1 = Top of the head
2 = Eyes
3 = Nose, shaped like a triangle

4 =	Forearms (crossed in front of you)
5 =	Fingers
6 =	Shoulders (hold three fingers up over each shoulder)
7 =	Seventh heaven on the back
8 =	What I ate (rub the stomach)
9 =	Knees
10 =	10 toes

To teach the planets, students simply connect each planet to its appropriate location on the body, such as imagining dirt being on their nose, to remember that the earth is the third planet from the sun.

We can combine the peg system with other memory strategies to improve recall of any subject—even spelling—as this next lesson shows.

LESSON 4

Memorizing information through rhyming, repetition, and writing new lyrics

Topic	Spelling
Students	First Grade: ages 6–7
Primary Green Light strategy	Memory
Related strategies	Tone, movement, and novelty
Submitted by	Shari Rindels, First-Grade Teacher
	Catalina Ventura School
	Phoenix, Arizona

Red Light. Traditionally, teachers have students practice their spelling words by sounding them out, spelling them letter by letter, writing them down three times each, writing each word in a sentence, and so forth. Students get easily bored and can quickly lose focus.

Green Light. As my class was chanting their favorite poem to help them learn directions—"North, south, east, west, first graders are the best!"—I got an idea to use this compass poem in a memory/peg activity as they learned to spell their weekly words. I gave them each a laminated 4- × 6-inch index card with a picture of a compass on it, complete with the letters N, S, E, and W printed on it. We practiced touching the letters as we said our poem, and then I told them how we could use this to learn to spell our weekly words. They looked at me as if I had two heads.

So I began to show them how the first letter is said as they touch the N, the second letter as they touch the S, the third letter as they touch the E, the fourth letter as they touch the W, and the whole word as they touch the middle. For shorter words, they just say the word at the direction that comes next. If the word contains a two-letter phonogram, such as wh, ee, or a double consonant, they say both letters together on one direction point. For example:

wheel	N = wh	S = ee	E = l	W =	"wheel"
four	N = f	S = ou	E = r	W =	"four"
catch	N = c	S = a	E = t	W = ch	"catch"
middle	N = m	S = i	E = dd	W = le	"middle"

They caught on quickly, and we use it to practice our words every Thursday. On test day, they may have their compasses out if they wish.

Effectiveness. The students are successfully learning both their more difficult words and their two-letter phonograms. In addition, spelling test scores have gone up dramatically for my at-risk students and my normally low spellers. Students even started predicting what compass point the word would end up on, for example, "I think *fur* is going to be a south word." The students' map skills have also improved. It has turned out to be a great tool. Our chant on Spelling Compass days is now always, "North, south, east, west, first-grade spellers are the best!"

DEBRIEF OF LESSON 4

This seemingly simple lesson actually contains three distinct memory strategies. The first is the rhyme, which is connected to the compass. When did Columbus sail the ocean blue? If you can recall the rhyme, you know the time (1492). Rhyming can assist students' recall by creating an easily remembered trigger to a cascade of information or ideas related to a topic. Rhyming devices can range from being as simple as the one in this demonstration, to two lines reflecting related pieces of information, to a full-blown poem covering an entire body of information. Student-created rhymes tend to be easiest for students to remember and add an entertaining dimension to any lesson.

Rhyming is also a key ingredient of most songs, and music can be used to trigger memories in a wide variety of ways. Have you ever heard a song and felt it connect to a very specific memory? As a memory device, one strategy would be to teach a particular topic and tie it directly to a song. Another idea might be to play songs where the lyrics match the topic. You could also have students rewrite the lyrics to a well-known song using key words from a lesson; then to remember the content, they would only need to hum a few bars from the song in their heads.

However, in this lesson, the playful rhyme is merely the starting point of the learning. In the second part, the students use movement to learn their letters. Movement engages our *muscle* or *procedural memory*—literally a memory learned through movement. Procedural memory is one of the most lasting forms, meaning that if we learn a task by physically doing it, it tends to stay with us for a long time. Current research (Paulin, 2005) suggests this may be because muscle movement triggers glucose production and engages far more neurons than simple cognitive tasks such as adding. Thus, literally acting out information increases the chances learning will be recalled.

The third strategy this teacher is using is review, yet in a fun and creative way. In other words, she's using repetition. Repetition helps recall. Repetition helps recall a lot. Repetition helps recall *quite* a lot, actually. (Enough already?) However, repetition is not a very popular technique for remembering information because most people believe it's boring, thinking, "I've already done this, why should I do it again?"

So to use repetition successfully in the classroom, Green Light teachers *vary* the way it is done. There are many ways to vary how you repeat material in your learning environment. Some examples might include asking learners to make a checklist, make a crossword puzzle, write a practice exam, teach it to another person, create some acronyms, illustrate the information, create a PowerPoint presentation, look information up on the Internet, do a small group review, create summary statements, or play the Expert and Doubter game. Also consider using pre-exposure, vocabulary builders, games, activities, advance organizers, field trips, previews, educational videos, pretesting, foreshadowing, priming . . .

For repetition to work best, we need to use it *after* error correction: we want students to repeat the *right* information! We also need to try to use repetition when students are in a variety of emotional states, but particularly in states of moderate to high stress to match the testing state. Finally, if possible, repetition should occur in the actual test location.

Hopefully, you'll find many of the lessons in this book unique or unusual, and that is intentional. Things that are unique stay in our memory longer. This final lesson plays to that concept.

LESSON 5

Memorizing information through novelty

Topic	Names of Cell Parts
Students	Fifth Grade: ages 10–11
Primary Green Light strategy	Memory
Related strategies	Novelty, movement, and socialization
Submitted by	Emma Jeter, Fifth-Grade Teacher
	Christopher Farms Elementary School
	Virginia Beach, Virginia

Red Light. Traditionally, we would draw a cell. I would give the students the labels and they would use the textbook to figure out what the job of each cell was. We would look at some cells under a microscope. Then they would create a diagram of a plant cell and an animal cell.

Green Light. We memorized our cell pegs and had already looked at some cells under a microscope. Then we had a lesson where we made *edible plant cells*. The students had graham crackers, icing, and assorted candies. Each of them had a fact sheet that gave them information about the different parts of the cell and what job they did. They chose to use the ingredients in any way they wanted. They had to create a cell with a cell wall, a cell membrane, a vacuole, a nucleus, and chloroplasts. Once they created their cell, they came and talked to me. They had to tell me what each part of their creation was and what job it did in the cell. They also had to tell me what would have been different if we had created animal cells (no cell wall and no chloroplast). Then they had to eat any parts of their cell that were not part of an animal cell. They came and showed me that, and then they could eat the rest of their cell.

As a follow-up to this lesson, I had them make a human plant cell with their bodies. They made the cell wall and cell membrane by sitting or lying on the floor of the classroom. We had two people form the vacuole. Some other students wore green shirts, and they were the chloroplasts. We had one individual wear a top hat to be the nucleus. Each person formed a different part of the cell, and we reviewed what their job was. I told the students that they had to know about this because the cell inspector was coming to town. We played Inspector Gadget music to get in the mood. Then I had another teacher dress up as the cell inspector, and he came in to interview them about their jobs. He made it really funny. The kids had a great time!

Effectiveness. Students still talk about this lesson. They talked to each other about the lesson. They told their friends about the lesson. They went home and talked about it with their parents. I had many parents come and tell me how much fun their children had and how much information about cells that they had shared at home! They love to recall how much fun we had. If I ask any of the students, they can easily tell me the parts and functions of a cell.

DEBRIEF OF LESSON 5

Novelty, while a Green Light strategy by itself, is also a key component to remembering information better. We tend to forget things that are usual, things we've seen many times over and over. Right now, try to remember what you ate for dinner exactly two weeks ago. If you can't remember, it's probably because there wasn't anything special or unusual about it. If you can, most likely there's something that stands out in your mind, such as the location, someone you ate with, or perhaps something that happened during the meal.

If a lesson is novel, intriguing, or fascinating, students will focus on it and pay attention at a higher level than they would to a typical Red Light lesson. This higher level of attention alone gives them a better chance of remembering the information.

In this lesson, the idea of eating their lesson was radical to the students. In fact, the idea of eating their "cells" was so unusual it prompted them to tell everyone else about what had happened. This is also very important. Every time the students related the lesson to another person, they built their memory of the content—they reviewed it, unprompted. Novelty frequently makes this happen. Students enjoy the lesson, so they remember it more, and they tell others about it, which further increases their memory.

Novelty doesn't have to be complex or difficult: we can achieve it by something as simple as humor. When Green Light teachers use humor, students often talk later about that moment in the classroom—again, reviewing the content.

Talking Does Not Mean Teaching

Teachers are often frustrated when students fail to remember content that has been discussed in class. If your students have ever asked, "When did you teach us that?" or if no amount of revision improves test results, try some of the memory strategies modeled in this chapter and, actually, throughout this book. Every chapter, every strategy, is designed to do one thing: help students remember material better. Specifically, they'll remember better if

- It's relevant to them
- They get to move their bodies
- The lesson is somehow novel
- The lesson includes sound or music
- They are emotionally involved in the lesson
- They get to talk to each other to process the information
- They get to act out the lesson
- They get to create some visuals

The point is, we can increase the chances of students remembering information if we both deliberately *employ* some of these techniques and then *explain* to our students why the techniques work and how to create their own.

Bear in mind, none of these strategies are meant to replace the actual teaching process. They only *support* students' ability to retain and recall the information. Green Light teachers would first want to look carefully at the material, isolate the key facts within the content that students most need to know, and consider how best to teach so these facts are more easily

memorable to the students. From that point, all the natural rhythms of the teaching process take over.

That said, while memory strategies are just one aspect of teaching, they are absolutely vital. Teaching without memory strategies is like sending our students on a scuba dive without first showing them how to use the regulator: some will figure it out themselves and enjoy the experience; most will be lucky just to survive. Understanding *how* to remember information is an essential learning skill. By empowering all students with that skill, Green Light teachers give every child the chance to achieve outstanding results in education.

KEY POINTS

- Students need to be taught how to remember information, not merely be expected to know how to do this on their own. It is a *skill* they can be taught.
- Teachers need to consciously choose a memory strategy that might fit a particular piece of content.
- Students of *all ages*, not just younger ones, need these memory strategies.

- The use of *association* is one of the most simple, and yet most powerful, memory devices.
- Acronyms and acrostics are two of the more common memory devices.
- Many types of content can be encoded in *stories* that include central points.
- Students often remember stories better if *they* make them up.
- Memory *pegs* can help students recall key facts within dense amounts of content.
- The body location method is a useful strategy for younger children.
- Repetition is most useful if *variety* is used each time the material is revisited.
- Many of the Green Light strategies in this book can assist memory, such as novelty, movement, sound, and social interaction.
- Simply saying something isn't enough—teachers must do more if they hope students will encode the information.

QUESTIONS TO ASK YOURSELF

- What are key facts from this content area that students need to know?
- What strategy fits for this particular age group?
- What strategy fits for this particular material?
- Could the students be given the chance to create their own strategies?

Useful Books About Memory and Memory Strategies

Your Memory. Kenneth L. Higbee. Marlowe, 2001.

Improving Your Memory. Richard McAndler. Gill & MacMilliam, 2002.

Use Your Perfect Memory. Tony Buzan. Penguin Books, 1990.

The Great Memory Book. Karen Markowitz & Eric Jensen. Corwin Press, 1999.

Kevin Trudeau's Mega Memory. Kevin Trudeau. William Morrow, 1995.

Remember Everything You Read. Stanley D. Frank. Random House, 1990.

Don't Forget. Danielle Lapp. Addison-Wesley, 1987.

Memory. Elizabeth Loftus. Addison-Wesley, 1980.

The Complete Idiot's Guide to Improving Your Memory. Michael Kurland & Richard Lupoff. Alpha Book, 1999.

Total Memory Workout: 8 Easy Steps to Maximum Memory Fitness. Cynthia R. Green. Bantam, 1999.

3 Connections

Connections link learning to life.

How will you use them in your lessons?

ADAPT . . . ADJUST . . . APPLY

Does this happen in your classroom? Every new subject is introduced through a link to the students' interests. Connections are made to the important people in their lives, to their weekend activities, to the physical world around them, and to current events. As far as students are concerned, content is always *relevant* to their world.

CONNECTIONS: AN OVERVIEW

When students learn new information, when they are first introduced to a new topic, their most common question is, "So what?" They wonder *why* they have to learn it, *what* could be so important about it, and *how* it could possibly be relevant to them. If the answers to these questions take too long to emerge, students mentally disengage, since—from their point of view—it obviously has nothing to do with them. Regardless of the motivational strategies or reward techniques a teacher may use, many students will still fail to engage with the content for a very simple reason: they don't care (Wells & Arauz, 2006).

The current educational system often insists that students learn what *appears* to be irrelevant information, and students react accordingly, with apathy, indifference, and even irreverence. The key word here is *appears*. When Red Light teachers allow their students to believe the information they are being forced to learn is extraneous, students switch off. This can have devastating consequences to their current motivation to learn, as well as their long-term readiness for life as an adult.

Green Light teachers find ways to connect the material they are teaching to the world of their students. They understand that material should be taught in ways that reflect their intimate connections in the world beyond education. They consider issues such as how this topic is connected—similar, comparable, or analogous—to anything students may have experienced. How can it be coupled with something they are familiar with? How can it be linked to something they already know, recognize, and enjoy? If the teacher can establish the starting point of a strong connection, students have an anchor to hold onto during the subsequent onslaught of new material.

Well-meaning teachers often make the mistake of connecting new information to previous information *within the same content area*. This can be a serious error because it may be perceived by students as piling yet more weight on top of an already shaky foundation. Instead . . .

The key is to make the connection *lateral*.

Associate the idea to something with which students may already be at ease, *outside* that content area. For example, if they aren't comfortable with math to begin with, they are going to be even *more* uncomfortable with learning *more* math! Therefore, Green Light teachers connect new concepts to something beyond this particular content area, something about which students already feel confident.

It is important to clarify the two distinct types of learning connections. One kind is the importance that *we*—as teachers—know this information holds for their futures. The other kind is what *they*—as students—perceive as relevant to their lives. Often teachers' focus is on the first kind, trying desperately to help students see the value they will gain by mastering the material. But students, going through their own stages of development, can rarely see further than today, beyond their friends, family, or personal interests. Teachers who miss this critical distinction often feel frustrated with the lack of interest students demonstrate for the topic—despite their best efforts to show students "how useful algebra will be" when they're an adult. Instead, we need to put away our own perception of the situation and use the second type of connection to engage our students' motivation, curiosity, and excitement.

The point is that connecting learning to things students already under-stand creates *relevance*. If it's relevant, they're interested and want to know more, because it's something real within their world. This has been demonstrated to great effect in Australia's remote Aboriginal communities where low literacy rates have been linked to a lack of relevant teaching materials.

As a visitor to a remote community, Victoria University education lec-turer Lawry Mahon noted, "there was an absolute lack of Aboriginal faces in class books and kids' stories. Most of the school books contained only white faces, white kids, white stories." It struck Lawry Mahon that the children would do far better with literacy resources that told their own sto-ries. This was the start of Story Writing in Remote Locations (SWIRL),* a program where Aboriginal students improve their literacy skills by com-posing their own stories and turning them into teaching resources. In every SWIRL location, students have improved their literacy, have been eager to learn, and have developed a renewed enthusiasm for attending school, with attendance rates jumping from 50 percent to 100 percent every time the program is run. All this because someone let the students read about something *relevant*.

Such is the power of relevance that Green Light teachers consciously and deliberately incorporate connections that engage students' minds in the classroom to help them become better learners. This first lesson takes that idea and puts it directly into practice. It provides a clear model of how

---

* SWIRL is sponsored by IBM and run by the Victorian University of Technology. For more infor-mation, visit http://www.ibm.com/ibm/ibmgives/grant/education/programs/swirl.shtml.

to make this potentially "conceptual" notion of building connections work on a very concrete level for the students.

LESSON 1

Connecting abstract content to something tangible

Topic	Fractions: "Sharing the Sandwich"
Students	First and Second Grades: ages 6–8
Primary Green Light strategy	Connections
Related strategies	Visuals, novelty, and emotion
Submitted by	Shari Rindels, First-Grade Teacher
	Catalina Ventura School
	Phoenix, Arizona

Red Light. Traditionally, a teacher would show students what equal parts, ½, and ¼ look like and then hand students a worksheet with shapes showing equal parts, halves, or fourths—whichever concept was being taught that day. The worksheet would show both correct and incorrect answers. The students would be directed to find and circle the "correct" pictures of a particular fraction.

Green Light. Trying to find a way to connect concepts to real life for my students—both my English and my non-English speakers—can be a challenge. However, in this unit I have found that all students seem to understand the concept of sandwiches, so I use them as the framework when teaching fractions.

I give each student a few slices of bread, a paper plate, a plastic knife, and a small container of peanut butter. I introduce the lesson by showing students my own favorite kind of sandwich: peanut butter, of course! I tell them I am not hungry enough to eat all of it and ask them for ideas on what I could do so that I don't waste it. The unanimous answer is for me to share it. So I put it on my overhead projector, which is a great visual, and proceed to cut it in half. However, I do *not* cut it into equal parts, and the kids all shout, "No fair, the pieces aren't the same size!" "Exactly," I say. "You have just discovered the secret to fractions—*equal parts*, which means having each part be the same size." So I slide the sandwich together and cut it correctly.

Next I start the guided practice part of the lesson by having them take a piece of bread and cut it into two equal parts. We practice cutting the equal parts both horizontally and vertically. We then talk about how they cut the bread in half, explaining that the word *half* means *two equal parts*. I both write and draw the fraction ½ on the overhead and talk about what those numbers mean. At this point, I have the students spread peanut butter on one half of their bread and eat it if they wish—waste not, want not! Being involved this way with the lesson makes it truly meaningful for them.

For demonstrating fractions with circles, I use tortillas and cheese, and we make quesadillas—a food my students relate to well here in the Southwest!

Effectiveness. One hundred percent participation! One hundred percent retention of the ideas of equal parts, halves, and fourths! One hundred percent scores on tests! When taught this way, I have yet to have a student *not* understand fractions.

DEBRIEF OF LESSON 1

This lesson demonstrates a wonderful connection between the potentially abstract concept of fractions and the very concrete idea of food. Food is something students are experienced with even at this young age, so the information they are learning is connected to something *real*, something *solid*, something *tangible* (Prensky, 2005). Green Light teachers look for what is real about the subject they are teaching and make those connections overt for the students.

It's easy to imagine how a teacher might present this concept in a way that would be difficult to understand, and how students might struggle to learn it. Fractions may well be perceived by students of this age as being an absurdly abstract concept, *unless taught properly*. However, even these young learners can process information at this level of abstraction, if a solid connection is built between the concept they are learning and a concrete reality in their world. Food is definitely something these kids understand, know, and like! And they are all familiar with the concept of sharing. By bringing together the real with the abstract, the teacher has found a way to present the idea so students can get a truly manageable grasp on it. The absolute importance of allowing students to get a firm grip on a lesson is demonstrated next.

LESSON 2

Connecting abstract content to physical artifacts

Topic	Civil Rights
Students	Fifth–Twelfth Grades: ages 10–18
Primary Green Light strategy	Connections
Related strategies	Movement, memory, visuals, and emotion
Submitted by	Keil Hileman, Eighth-Grade Teacher
	Monticello Trails Middle School
	Shawnee, Kansas

Red Light. Students have usually read textbook articles and done worksheets. If they were lucky, they may have had a classroom discussion, watched a video clip, or done a research paper on slavery and civil rights. When taught this way, most students are not capable of understanding the horrors of slavery or the significance of our civil rights.

Green Light. I have made it both a passion and a mission to collect any artifact that helps my students connect with the concepts of slavery and civil rights. I begin by showing the first 20 minutes of the movie *Amistad*. I have tracked down real and reproduction slave shackles that I then allow students to wear. Their "intellectual eyes" are truly opened when they feel the heavy cold metal on their wrists and ankles, and realize how restricted the slaves truly were when wearing these brutal constraints.

In addition, I have a slave ball and chain that was made from a Civil War Era ship cannon ball. All students are given an opportunity to put it on, drag it around the room, and see how easy it is to still do their "chores." My sixth-grade students are barely able to lift it off the ground, and none of my eighth-grade students can hold the ball up for more than two minutes. They are literally holding the "weight of history" in their own two hands.

The past few years, I have learned about and collected many varieties of slave trade beads. These were used by Europeans to trade for human beings in and around Africa for the past 500 years. They come in many types, although the most valuable ones are the tiny cobalt blues. Fourteen cobalt blues would have bought you a human being. If you saw a man with many strands of blue beads, you knew he was a slave trader, and you stayed away. I have several reproductions of these in my room for students to touch, hold, and explore kinesthetically.

I have my students touch all these items, and I tell stories about them. Eventually, students write their own stories involving these artifacts. In the end, it is the physical contact with these artifacts that helps them make a very real connection to—and thus understand—their civil rights, slavery, and the history of the slave trade.

Effectiveness. This teaching strategy sets my students on fire. They are alive, interested, intrigued, and drawn in, because they now have a beginning point for understanding the emotional experience of the slaves. Sometimes they are even horrified when learning about these objects, yet this emotion is perfectly appropriate since slavery was such a horrific chapter in human history. By touching the artifacts, by making physical contact with the reality of the topic, students' emotions are fired up, and they *want to know more*!

DEBRIEF OF LESSON 2

The idea of civil rights could have been—and often still is—taught using a very dry, textbook-oriented approach. However, this innovative teacher chose to make it significantly more real to students by connecting it to physical, tangible artifacts. By having an opportunity to hold, wear, and kinesthetically discover the true nature of these items, the subject immediately becomes real. It suddenly jumps from being a two-dimensional, abstract idea into a three-dimensional, full-blown, in-their-face reality (Wilson, 2004).

Red Light teachers might believe that using artifacts is only relevant when teaching history, yet almost all subject areas have physical objects associated with them. For example, in English class, the related artifacts might be old books, pens, or reading lamps. Math artifacts might be slide rulers, adding machines, abacuses, or even early pocket calculators. Geography artifacts might include old maps, different *types* of maps, or photos and models of different types of terrains. The opportunities are truly endless. The bottom line is:

Toys teach!

By creating relevance through the use of artifacts, Green Light teachers can unfurl the sails of possibility that exist within any topic and set sail on a dynamic, multidimensional learning experience with their students. When the subject *matters*, when it's important, it becomes imperative to students to know more. When students make these types of connections, they are truly engaged in the learning process.

The idea of linking learning to an external entity can even be extended further, past the use of physical objects, to *processes* that students recognize and understand.

LESSON 3

Connecting patterns, sequences, or procedures to real-life processes

Topic	The Writing Process: "Baby Food Day"
Students	Third–Fifth Grades: ages 8–11
Primary Green Light strategy	Connections
Related strategies	Visuals and novelty
Submitted by	Tina Bernard, Gifted and Talented Specialist
	Mound Elementary School
	Burleson, Texas

Red Light. Traditionally, when asked to write a composition, students often will grumble, moan, and whine—while the more inventive ones will ask to go to the nurse. Sitting there with blank stares, they glumly begin planning how they will respond to the prompt and—feeling overwhelmed—the tears begin. Much to the surprise of the teacher (who usually anticipates brilliance), the pages are filled with grammatical errors and very mundane writing. After hours of editing, the essays are returned by the frustrated teacher, asking students to make corrections and turn the assignment back in when they have "fixed" it. The teacher wonders what she is doing wrong—and students feel the same!

Green Light. To begin teaching a writing lesson, I bring in pictures of my baby and a few jars of baby food. I open one of them and walk around eating it while telling students all about my precious family. As disgusting as it may sound, the kids are completely engrossed in what I am doing, although not exactly in what I am saying. Soon, however, I draw in their attention by explaining to them the feeding of infants, saying,

> You begin by feeding them only peaches. You do this for a few days, and if all goes well, you introduce something else. However, if there is an allergic reaction to the peaches, you know exactly what the problem is. If all is well, you can move on and try something new—bananas, for instance. You eventually move on and begin to combine foods, but not until a regular feeding pattern is established. Using this approach, very soon you can have them eating an entire fruit salad.

Then I equate that with the writing process. Slowly, paragraph by paragraph, we work through an essay. I explain, saying,

> I will not let you move on to the next paragraph until I know for sure the paragraph that you are invested in is excellent. If there is a problem, or if something is giving you grief, then we need to work together to fix the problem while we can. It would sure be sad to have a whole essay that doesn't work just because we tried to make fruit salad rather than first enjoy the taste of the peaches.

As students begin to complete their first paragraph they raise their hands and I mark their papers using a *peach-colored pen*, to represent peaches. They then move on to the "bananas" paragraph. This is a quick way to check the status of the class and ensure quality at all times during the writing process. Students then work on only one part of the essay at a time using a small, separate sheet of paper for each paragraph. Finally, when they are ready, they ask, "Can I make my fruit salad?" In my classroom, that means their story is ready to have the paragraphs put together to form a single composition. We top it off with some "whipped cream": reading it aloud!

Effectiveness. I can more effectively and efficiently work with students when they are engaged and self-assured, rather than hesitant and unsuccessful. Equating the writing process to something understandable seems to make them much more confident. Using this sequential approach, they tend to enjoy the experience of writing a composition, as they move carefully forward from one success to the next. When the cycle is complete, the compositions are usually quite beautiful and contain very few errors—while the self-esteem of the class is through the roof.

DEBRIEF OF LESSON 3

Many events in life occur sequentially, in a logical step-by-step manner, and it is the cumulative effect of the *process* that creates the intended result. The idea of a careful linear progression—one thing building upon another—is also fundamental to the understanding of many classroom topics. Often there are underlying patterns to the information, or clear steps that should be followed, but the point of emphasis during a lesson is on the *facts* alone. In teaching composition writing, for example, Red Light teachers would most likely focus on the grammar or sentence structure. While these issues are certainly important, the underlying *sequence of steps* is even more important, as it provides the basis of comfort and understanding from which students can venture forth and learn at the next level when they are ready.

Many things that we now do automatically, we learned sequentially, and sometimes it's important to remind students of this fact. Tying shoelaces is automatic to most of us, yet when we first "studied" it, the topic was highly complex, and we approached it one careful step at a time. When choosing what to use as a connection to new content, if it is something students view as being *automatic*—or at least *easy*—this can give them a confidence boost. If they see the original process as undemanding and painless, they are more likely to say, "If I learned to do *that*, maybe I can learn to do *this*!"

Isolating and highlighting any patterns, sequences, or processes within new material can be essential when teaching many subjects. If students can connect the new information to a similar process within their range of familiarity, their understanding of the entire unit will rise automatically. They will use the connection as a blueprint from which to construct their knowledge and understanding of the subject. Once a suitable connection to the pattern has been established and reinforced, students have already learned a sizable amount of the information.

The theme of making connections between classroom concepts and external events and processes can be adjusted as needed, depending on the nature of the content. In this next example, the focus of the connection is on something all students experience every day—the physical environment of the school building.

LESSON 4

Connecting content to the physical environment beyond the classroom

Topic	Art: "Lines in School"
Students	Second and Third Grades: ages 7–9
Primary Green Light strategy	Connections

Related strategies	Movement, tone, and novelty
Submitted by	Sheryl Fainges, Year 2 Teacher
	Manly West State School
	Manly West, Queensland, Australia

Red Light. Teaching students the use of lines in art would normally involve the use of blank paper, pencils, and crayons. The teacher would draw a thin line or a thick line on the board, and the students would proceed to copy it. The teacher would then venture into curved lines, jagged lines, soft lines, and hard lines. Each time, students would mirror the actions of the teacher.

Green Light. The "Lines in School" lesson is developed around making connections to the physical school environment. I first use a digital camera to walk around the building, taking photos of various types of lines in the environment, both man-made and natural. Man-made lines might include brickwork, wood seating, stairs, chain-wire fencing, and louvers. Natural lines might include leaves, tree bark, tree rings, rocks, and flowers. These images are used to create handouts for a scavenger hunt, where students work in pairs to identify the source of the lines.

During the scavenger hunt, students walk around with paper and crayon and make rubbings of the various surfaces (lines) they encounter. Impressions can be made of the leaves, wood, and so forth. Students can also sketch what they see—for example, the wooden seats or the bark of the tree. An extension challenge I sometimes offer students is asking them to discover and point out *new* lines within their environment, or perhaps even create an environmental journal. Students are encouraged to develop their observational skills and an eye for detail. A final level of this lesson sometimes involves the students being given my digital camera and being encouraged to take their own photographs of other lines at school.

Effectiveness. Teaching the concept of lines in art this way establishes meaning for my students. The activity is seen as relevant because they can make connections with their own environment as they develop their new awareness of lines of all kinds. Language, art, and science can be naturally integrated into this process as students freely discuss their findings. Normally disengaged students become thoroughly engaged in this lesson, and are often the ones seen running from one spot to another just to be the first to discover the next line, the first to make the next connection!

DEBRIEF OF LESSON 4

In this lesson, the teacher is connecting a classroom concept to physical objects within their everyday environment. Not only does this strategy expand students' understanding of the *application* of the concept, but at the highest level this really is why the lesson is being taught! They are learning about lines because they are not just some vague idea; lines really are an important part of their world.

Red Light teachers sometimes forget the need for this higher level of teaching and learning, keeping concepts and ideas tucked tightly into the theoretical realm. Whenever possible, content should be deliberately connected to the environment beyond the walls of the classroom, beyond the ramparts of the school, beyond the boundaries of cities, states, and countries, as much as possible broadening students' understanding of the concept to encompass the entire world. It is the world they live in, and the more thoroughly they understand how it works, the better off they will be to live within it.

This strategy also incorporates a wonderful hidden benefit: given how they were taught the concept—and the connections they established to the physical world around them—every time students see these objects in the future, they will be reminded of the lesson. They may even proudly point out lines to their friends or family. By doing this, they are essentially reviewing the material, cementing their knowledge firmly in place without realizing it. Whenever students can be mentally engaged on a pragmatic, down-to-earth level, they learn more naturally and easily as they form positive connections to the concept.

Of course, to many teenagers, the most important thing in *their* world is their peers. This next lesson takes advantage of this basic fact of teen life.

LESSON 5

Connecting content to the students' social environment

Topic	Population Estimation: "Catch and Release"
Students	High school: ages 14–18
Primary Green Light strategy	Connections
Related strategies	Socialization, novelty, and movement
Submitted by	Rob Jensen, Earth Science and Biology Teacher
	Hellgate High School
	Missoula, Montana

Red Light. The traditional way of presenting this idea, extolled in many textbooks as a "hands-on" application of the concept, is to repetitively mark and "recapture" beans in a jar. The number of beans is estimated by equating the ratios of marked to unmarked beans with the number originally marked. This, of course, makes the students "bean counters," which I simply won't allow in my classroom!

Green Light. I start by challenging students to brainstorm a way to estimate our school's *student* population. They are then informed that the next morning I will "capture" students in other teachers' classes, "mark" them with orange flagging, and "release" them at the period's end. I usually mark about 10 percent of the student body. Students then brainstorm a written procedure that uses this information.

The next day, several student procedures are run concurrently. For example, each student can "capture" the students in their classes throughout the day, count those who are marked, and pool their data with the other students'. Each method is later checked against school attendance data for accuracy, and we discuss the assumptions, biases, and accuracy of each method. Now that they've made a real-life connection between the student population and the general concept of population estimation, they easily understand the "mark-recapture" method commonly used by wildlife biologists.

Effectiveness of Strategy: I tried it the traditional way...once. My students thought it was tedious and boring. They were not engaged because they honestly didn't care how many beans were in the jar. (Would you?) With a *student* population and using a method *they've* developed, enthusiasm was off the charts, and so were the number of correct answers on the homework and test!

DEBRIEF OF LESSON 5

Given that this teacher works in Montana, where fishing is a popular sport, even the *title* of the lesson will connect with many students. The expression "catch and release" is frequently associated with fishing, so the phrase—and the general concept—will already be familiar to many students. A creative, imaginative title to a lesson can capture students' attention at the beginning of class and provide an initial connection for teachers to build on. Students start off feeling as if this material will be something they know at least a *little* bit about.

The lesson builds on this confidence by engaging students with one of their most important issues: their sense of self-identity, and consequently their relationship to their peers. By making a connection between the concept he is teaching and a topic that is of great concern—the students and their *social* environment—the chances they will understand the material soar (Wells & Arauz, 2006).

Whenever teachers establish a link between the content they are teaching and issues students are already interested in, student motivation takes a great step forward. Fortunately, students are actually interested in a wide range of issues, beyond their peers. Whatever has significance or importance or is of consequence to them is fair game for teachers to use when making connections. The emotional power of the issue tends to transfer to the content area. When this happens, students make a good start toward effective learning.

THE CRITICAL NATURE OF CONNECTIONS

Our education systems should prepare our children for life, for becoming successful and contributing members of society. Yet how many students would agree that schools achieve this objective? Most would say school is merely something to be survived before moving on to more useful or practical pursuits. Tying content to real life allows students to see at least some level of connection between their school experience and the bigger world.

The simple truth is that a lack of relevance to what they are learning may be the single most influential reason students lack interest, enthusiasm, and inspiration in the classroom. By using connections, associations, and other links to life, Green Light teachers can create a higher level of *meaning* for students. These relationships ultimately make their school experience more practical, pertinent, and applicable to their future.

KEY POINTS

- Connections establish the *relevance* of the content.
- Without meaning, there is no real learning.
- Lateral connections to things *outside* the current content area are important.
- Look for what is real about a subject—how it is a part of the physical world—and make those connections *overt* for students.
- Connect learning processes to processes students either can understand easily or already know.
- If the connection is with something students perceive as easy, they are more likely to believe that learning the new content will be easy as well.
- When connections are made to the physical world around them, every time they see the object it will remind them of the lesson and cement the learning.
- When possible, use connections to issues that are naturally of interest and concern to students.
- An original *title* to a lesson can create a great opening connection.
- Connections, associations, and links bring learning to life. When *why* they are learning new material makes sense to students, they feel it's worth the investment of their time, energy, and resources to learn it.

QUESTIONS TO ASK YOURSELF

- How can you occasionally provide *lateral* connections for students? How would you adjust this idea to make it effective in your classroom?
- Where might "artifact teaching" fit in your content area, or with the grade level of the students you work with? Where can you gather more artifacts?

- How can you make content that appears "conceptual" to students more "real," more grounded in the world around them and their experiences?
- What processes do your students frequently forget? How can you connect those processes to ones they already know?
- What are your students naturally interested in? How can you link your lessons to their concerns?

4 Movement

Movement magnifies learning.

How will you use them in your lessons?

ADAPT . . . ADJUST . . . APPLY

Does this happen in your classroom? Students are kept alert and comfortable by being physically engaged in the lesson at appropriate intervals. In addition to being given chances to stand and move about the classroom, activity is frequently an integral part of the learning process, with movements designed to convey core lesson content. A balance is always maintained between seated learning and physical engagement.

MOVEMENT: AN OVERVIEW

For many years, educators have believed that students learn best when they sit quietly at their seats—a belief that has given rise to the outdated models of "Drill and Kill" or "Chalk and Talk," or, as it's sometimes referred to in Texas, "Sit and Git"! While schools occasionally make "allowances" and permit movement in classes with younger students, there seems to be an unconscious rule that once students are "old enough," the more they can and should sit.

As a result, most middle school, high school, and certainly university students spend most of their learning time being *physically uncomfortable*. When students get uncomfortable in their chairs, what's their next reaction? The "fidget factor" sets in straight away, as they twist about in their chairs to relieve the dreaded condition known as "numb bum." The minute students pick up this condition, learning has ceased. They're not listening to the teacher anymore—they're just thinking, "Please, let me stand up, move around, and stretch my aching legs!"

As fast food restaurants know, people can't sit on a hard chair for very long. In fact, these restaurants deliberately choose the very same chairs we expect our students to sit on to encourage customers to eat and leave quickly. And it works! Try it yourself sometime: try sitting down in almost any fast food restaurant and relaxing and enjoying your meal for an hour. Chances are you'll be aching to get out of that seat and move within 15 to 20 minutes. Why do we expect our students to do any better?

So what's the answer? Give our students more comfortable chairs? Actually, no. Because for those lucky students who do get comfortable, learning is equally elusive: students become too relaxed to learn. Although they might be comfortable, students are not engaged, not fully processing new information, and not considering what it might mean to them. They mentally disconnect and begin to daydream or get sleepy.

The issue is, whether comfortable or not, if students sit too long, the body's natural processes slow down: blood begins to settle in their feet and backside, and less oxygen is transported to the brain. This physical state does *not* support learning. Oxygen is good for the brain! It helps the brain to function properly at its highest levels (Hannaford, 2005).

The answer is to get our students *moving*. As Green Light teachers, we must find ways to get students at least occasionally in motion, if for no other reason than to get their blood flowing. It's a simple equation:

Movement . . . *leads to* more oxygen in the brain . . . *leading to* better learning.

Deliberately stopping our students from moving may be the single most significant barrier to their learning and recalling new material (Jensen, 2002). Yet Red Light teachers resist movement for several reasons, the first and most common being that they are afraid of losing control—preferring instead the *illusion* of control they get from talking *at* a group of fidgeting students incapable of concentrating on the material.

Another reason Red Light teachers resist movement is the misapprehension that students who move while the teacher is talking are being rude or disruptive. But is that necessarily true? Think of your own experience: when you were a student, when you attended a presentation, or perhaps even during a faculty meeting, have *you* ever wanted to stand up and stretch, but felt that would somehow be wrong? You weren't meaning to be disruptive; you were just uncomfortable! How odd that it's *not* OK for someone to stand up while they are listening, but it *is* OK for them to sit in discomfort. This strange "rule" is so strongly ingrained that even adult learners require explicit permission to break it: the teacher must publicly announce, "It's OK with me if you want to stand up and stretch at any point during this class."

So how can we introduce movement into our classrooms in ways that don't just retain classroom control, but actually support the learning process? Green Light teachers have at least three options.

1. Give students permission to make themselves comfortable.

As Green Light teachers, we need to give students the explicit permission to make sure their bodies are comfortable, so they can maximize their learning. For example, a teacher who was trying to introduce small amounts of movement into his classroom simply informed students that—if they wanted to—when doing homework or a worksheet, they were allowed to stand at their desks and work. While it may seem awkward to work in that position, many students were willing to do it, simply because it gave them the chance to get out of their seats. They were willing to exchange the minor discomfort of working bent over for the relief of being able to stand up and stretch their legs, and get rid of their "numb bum"!

2. Bring movement into administrative activities.

Consider the issue of distributing handouts to students. The normal—Red Light—way of passing them out to students might be to hand them out one at a time, the teacher giving one to each student. Or maybe a stack is given to a student at the head of each row and then students pass them to other students behind them. Classic, usual, typical, and . . . completely static and boring! Instead, why not have the students stand up, and then toss the papers high into the air and let them fly out among them? Then the students can bend down and pick them up, making sure all students around them have one. Or perhaps even ask the students to toss the papers in the air! You've created an educational variation of the silly card game "52 Pick-up."

There's a good chance the suggestion above might be met with horror by some teachers, who may believe it's too radical—too *bright* Green! If so, use a milder variation: Simply stack the handouts in the back of the room. When it's time to distribute them, ask students to go pick up what they need. At least it will give them the opportunity—if only for a brief moment—to stand and stretch their legs.

The reader should know that all of these variations for "distributing resources" using movement have actually been used by the author with high school students, university students, and thousands of adults. While at first these learners often react with astonishment, they very quickly join in the game. They seem to recognize—whether consciously or unconsciously—the inherent value in being given the opportunity to engage their bodies during the learning process.

3. Bring physicality into the learning process.

An even more powerful means of getting the classroom moving is to bring physicality into the teaching process itself—making sure students never get to the point of needing to stand and stretch. While Red Light teachers only describe key ideas *verbally*, Green Light teachers know that verbal recall on its own can be a challenge for many learners. Instead, they find as many opportunities as possible to allow students to *physically* engage with the learning process.

We discussed this point, the idea of increasing recall by attaching specific content to "muscle" or "procedural" memories, in Chapter 2. The layer we are adding here is that, by bringing physicality into the teaching process, we are not only assisting recall; we are also relieving the discomfort of sitting on a hard chair and keeping the blood flowing to our students' brains.

Before we get to the demonstration lessons, let us be clear that allowing movement is not an invitation for the classroom to descend into anarchy:

OF COURSE teachers will occasionally want students to sit quietly at their desks or tables . . .

OF COURSE seated learning is an effective mode of learning for some instructional situations, and . . .

OF COURSE students must know how to do this, when needed.

However, as the following demonstration lessons show, in almost every aspect of the learning process, we can add a physical component to assist students in learning easily and effectively, while still retaining control of the classroom.

LESSON 1

Using action to teach subject areas not normally associated with movement

Topic	Spelling
Students	Fifth Grade: ages 10–11
Primary Green Light strategy	Movement
Related strategies	Socialization, memory, and novelty
Submitted by	Cindy Rickert, Fifth-Grade Teacher
	Christopher Farms Elementary School
	Virginia Beach, Virginia

Red Light. Traditionally, students are presented with a list of spelling words at the beginning of the week. The teacher then presents a lesson on the spelling pattern. Practice is done in the form of worksheets throughout the week. Students take a spelling test at the end of the week.

Green Light. To introduce the week's spelling words, I write each word on an index card and throw the stack of cards in the air. Students scramble to grab a card. Once they have a card, they get in line to "hop" out their word. I draw a 35-letter, 10-row letter hopscotch on my classroom floor (vowels and R, S, T, and N are written twice). Each box is approximately 12 inches square.

After each student hops out his or her word, the class praises the student. The spelling pattern for the week naturally shows up as each student hops out the word. Throughout the week, we practice the words by hopping on the letters.

Effectiveness. Since implementing this method of teaching, Friday spelling tests are now always a success. I often observe students looking at the letter hopscotch to remember how to spell the words.

Figure 4.1   Spelling Hopscotch Grid

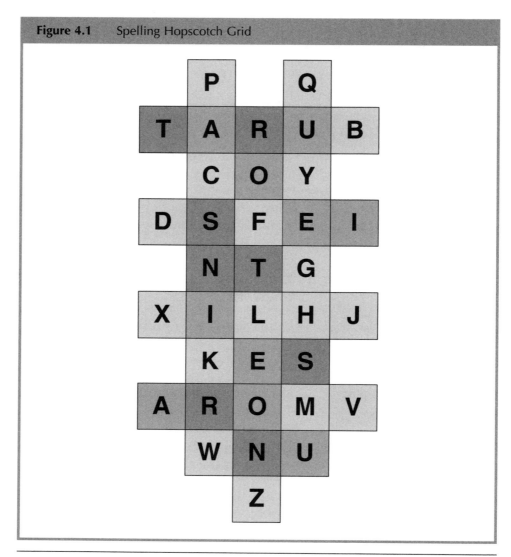

Source: Cindy Rickert, Christopher Farms Elementary, Virginia Beach, Virginia.

DEBRIEF OF LESSON 1

In this spelling lesson, students were learning the content through muscle movement. In the context of this book, the key learning is that, at first glance, the topic itself *doesn't seem to naturally lend itself to movement*. That will certainly be the case in many teaching situations: the content doesn't appear to be one where movement is a strategy that most teachers would consider using.

Despite this, Green Light teachers constantly search for ways to add movement to their teaching. This lesson, where students are connecting the movements to the spelling patterns, gives us an excellent place from which to start that search. Perhaps we can connect movements to other patterns? These might be simple numerical series like times tables, or more complex ideas such as the order of elements in the periodic table.

But movement doesn't just help with learning *patterns*. As Lesson 2 shows, we can also tie specific *actions* to specific *content*.

LESSON 2

Applying the concept of movement to almost any subject area

Topic	Math Concepts
Students	Eighth Grade: ages 13–14
Primary Green Light strategy	Movement
Related strategies	Memory and tone
Submitted by	Marcia Beldock, Eighth-Grade Teacher
	R. E. Simpson School
	Phoenix, Arizona

Red Light. Traditionally, the typical way to teach arithmetic and geometry is by worksheets. Some methods might use pencils or other objects to attempt to visually present the topics being taught.

Green Light. In my classroom, students understand that one of the best ways to remember concepts is by putting them "in" our muscles. I try to come up with a movement for all of our major concepts. For example, students model parallel, perpendicular, and intersecting lines. For the more complicated topics, we find "trigger" words and motions that trigger their memories. Sometimes I will even have them make up their own motions, and they love it! I have had students who have hated math in the past and now tell me, "This is the first time in my *whole* life that I have liked math!"

As an example, after discovering that my eighth graders had enormous problems doing arithmetic with decimals, I decided it was time to try something different. I first created numbered steps to solve the different problems. Then, as a class, we came up with *motions* that went with each numbered step. For example, the first step on adding decimals is to line up the decimals. The students demonstrate this by clapping their hands above their head and then "draw" that imaginary line straight down. They visualize the decimals being lined up.

For an added bit of fun, I gave these movements a humorous name. We call it "Belates." It is my last name meshed with karate. I joke with them that they can even use these movements as self-defense techniques. I get many requests for "Belates." It is also a great way to review different concepts in an enjoyable way!

Effectiveness. Belates has had a very positive effect on my classroom. It has not only helped my students remember the steps for solving equations, but also boosted their self-esteem and enthusiasm for math. During parent/teacher conferences, I had parents telling me that their children were teaching them Belates. I also got numerous comments on how the students were using Belates to complete their homework. One of our biggest achievements is that *every one in each of my classes has passed* the decimals quiz with a B or better. They felt very accomplished and had such a great time learning as well!

DEBRIEF OF LESSON 2

In the first lesson, spelling was the topic being covered by the teacher. Here, the subject is math—another area many people think of as "conceptual" and therefore difficult to teach with movement. Yet at its most fundamental level, math is one of humankind's attempts to describe and understand the physical universe. In other words, teaching it in a physical manner fits perfectly with what the material is all about! Teachers who want to help students understand why they are learning the material they are involved with would certainly want to teach math—at least partially—from a physical point of view.

For example, to take an extreme situation, it might be said that the majority of calculus is concerned with describing the rate of change in the two-dimensional area of a graph under an equation. (If you don't teach this and just said, "WHAT?" . . . that's fine. The important aspect of this example should still make sense.) One Green Light teacher chose to present the majority of this topic by providing each student in his class with a large chunk of clay. After students had created certain equations, they were required to use the clay to physically build a model of the area under the graph. They would then walk around the room, commenting on other students' creations. The reverse situation also occurred, where students would build a model out of clay, and other students would walk around and design an equation to describe the model. While this is a somewhat simplified explanation for what is a highly complex subject, the point is, this teacher is getting the concept across using clay building—and also finding a reason to get students walking around the room.

Another area of math content that appears vastly complex to many students is algebra. However, if it is taught at least occasionally in a physical manner, the subject can spring to life. One example here might be multiplying binomials. (Again, if this isn't your area of expertise, the point should still be easy enough to understand.) On paper, many students struggle to understand where each variable goes. However, it can be easily demonstrated physically, with chairs representing the parentheses, and students acting out each of the parts, walking to the various positions. Once most students have physically walked the examples once or twice, understanding frequently soars. Transferring this understanding to the worksheet aspect of multiplying binomials now becomes "exponentially" easier.

Of course this is not how math is usually taught. Once students get beyond counting and simple arithmetic, math is a paper-and-pencil subject. You may find that, if you remove these two crutches, your students may initially develop "paper-and-pencil separation anxiety." However, once learners experience quantum leaps in understanding through physical engagement, they will embrace this new teaching style with enthusiasm.

The subject of this discussion has been math. However, it could have been about many other subjects that also appear too conceptual to be taught through movement: English, science, history, or literature, for example. At first glance, it may seem daunting to figure out how to add movement into teaching these subjects. Yet it is possible to add physical engagement into almost every one of them (Pica, 2006).

Regardless of their subject, whenever possible, Green Light teachers try to engage their students physically, even in learning something as dry as an instructional objective—the subject of Lesson 3.

LESSON 3

Using physical movements to teach primarily verbal information

Topic	Learning the Self-Defense Course Objective
Students	High school girls: ages 14–18
Primary Green Light strategy	Movement
Related strategies	Memory and novelty
Submitted by	Karen Renaud, PE and Health Teacher
	Ashland High School
	Ashland, Massachusetts

Red Light. Students must memorize the instructional objective of the course. It is a quote that is rather meaningless to high school girls when we first begin. They don't really understand what it means and have a very difficult time memorizing it. It is a course requirement to know this quote:

To develop and enhance the options of self-defense so they may become viable considerations to the woman who is attacked.

When I took the course, the instructor read the quote and then told us to memorize it. So, I did what I had always done. I kept reading and repeating the quote over and over until I could remember it—which took a very long time.

Green Light. I tried the Red Light approach the first couple of times that I taught the course and—like me—my students had a very difficult time remembering it. Therefore, I decided to try attaching a physical movement to the words in the quote.

Now, I begin by reading the quote and explaining what it means. Then, students stand up and we simultaneously say and physically "do" the quote:

> To develop (hands come together as if you are making something) and enhance (a dramatic opening of the arms) the options (we point in the air as if we are seeing our options) of self-defense (we do several quick punches) so they may become viable (we bring hands toward shoulders ending in a strong bicep curl) considerations (we put our fingers on the chin and look as if we are considering something) to the woman (point to ourselves) who is attacked (make a classic knife-stabbing gesture).

We repeat this together several times, and then students work with a partner to ensure they know the entire sequence. I ask them to make their physical movements very big and dramatic while also emphasizing the words. We follow up by reviewing it once or twice together as a class. I now end almost all my classes by revisiting this quote.

Effectiveness. This gets an A+ from me and my students. Since I have begun doing this, I would say that students will typically learn this quote within 15 minutes. I believe it is because they have those physical triggers in their body. Many students think it isn't cool to do at first but later tell me that they have started using this physical movement technique to help them learn many types of information in other classes.

Another testament to the effectiveness of the strategy was from two of my students whom I sent to the self-defense instructor training course. These two students were 18 years old in a class of about 30 police officers. The officers were learning this information for the first time and were struggling with the quote. My students decided to teach the rest of the class how to learn the quote using our physical movement technique. It was a huge success, and they became the heroines of the instructor training course. Can you imagine my two high school girls leading a group of seasoned police officers through this? They were very proud.

DEBRIEF OF LESSON 3

The key point of this lesson is similar to that of Lesson 2. However, in this case, the teacher is using the physicality of the actions to specifically identify and isolate certain words in a sequence, rather than steps in a numerical process.

Notice how the teacher has *isolated precisely what the students need to know verbally*, and *attached movement in some form to these key facts, ideas, and concepts.* Sometimes, as in this lesson, the teacher can decide the actions in advance. However, it's also very powerful to invite students to create their own actions—and perhaps even share them with the rest of the class.

Notice also how the teacher uses the actions in later classes as a review. This also provides an opportunity to once again physically engage students in the learning process, or provide them with a "brain break," as described in Lesson 4.

LESSON 4

Aligning content to specific motions, actions, or movements

Topic	The Five Parts of a Friendly Letter
Students	Fifth Grade: ages 10–11
Primary Green Light strategy	Movement
Related strategies	Memory, novelty, and tone
Submitted by	Paul M. Jungel, Fourth-Grade Teacher
	R. E. Simpson School
	Phoenix, Arizona

Red Light. The standard poster on the wall tells students that there are five parts to a friendly letter. Teachers for decades have struggled to get their classes to memorize the standard "heading, greeting, body, closing, and signature" elements of the friendly letter. You can have the students write it out, fill in the blanks, and compose their own letters, but the red markers continue to come out and the corrections get made. Then you can have them write another, but often the results are very similar or only changed slightly.

Green Light. When getting students involved in writing a friendly letter, why not involve the whole child? That is to say, add some movement to the learning process and get that blood circulating and those creative juices flowing. This works wonders in my classroom, and anyone can do it in a matter of minutes. However, the impact of this learning will last a lifetime. I begin by having everyone stand up. Now, using my body, I say it like this:

- First part. While touching my head, I say, "This is the heading."
- Second part. I use my hands to mimic shouting and say, "This is the greeting."
- Third part. I run my hands and arms up the side of my body and say, "This is the body."

- Fourth part. I bring my legs together, crossing them, and say, "This is the closing." (This fourth part is probably the most memorable as we'd had a rash of "accidents" around the school with students not making it to the bathroom in time.)
- Fifth part. I use my foot to write my name in the air, as this is the signature.

Effectiveness. This may seem simple, but it has been very effective in teaching the five parts of the friendly letter. You can ask any student in my class to "demonstrate" the five parts of the friendly letter and, without exception, you'll see that this particular learning has been placed in their long-term memory. It's fun, fast, and forever ingrained in their minds. Why? Because it is different from what they are used to, it is outside the normal "box," and it demands movement. At this point, it is now a super "brain break" that can be utilized at any point in the school day, providing both movement and review.

DEBRIEF OF LESSON 4

In teaching the five parts of the friendly letter using movement, this teacher is aligning the content with specific hand motions and getting the order correct by making the actions move down the body (Zachopoulou, Trevlas, & Konstadinidou, 2006).

These initial four lessons give us a host of ideas for using movement to help students learn patterns, processes, and sequences. Lesson 5 takes this to the next level by using a game to teach a *theory*.

LESSON 5

Adapting kid games for use as physical teaching tools

Topic	Germs and Pathogens
Students	Third Grade: ages 8–9
Primary Green Light strategy	Movement
Related strategies	Tone, novelty, and drama
Submitted by	Kim Cooke, PE and Health Teacher
	Union County Schools
	Monroe, North Carolina

Red Light. Traditionally, the teacher talks about how germs can cause you to get sick and that washing hands in important. The teacher may read a story to the students on how to prevent you from getting sick.

Green Light. PE teachers often play a game called Freeze Tag in which students who get tagged by someone must freeze until they are rescued. In the gymnasium, I use the same activity to teach the Germs and Pathogens concept. Suppose I choose two students to become the pathogens and hand them each a small green bean bag or ball. I explain to the students that pathogens are disease-causing agents and can make us sick—YUCK! I then select two students to become the white blood cells and give them a jersey to wear to identify them as the "superheroes of the body system."

When the music starts (I use "Stayin' Alive" by the Bee Gees), the pathogens skip after the rest of the students and try to *touch* them with the green bean bag or ball (not *throw* it) to make them sick. If a student gets touched by the pathogen, he or she must stop skipping and yell "Save me, white blood cells, save me!" Once a white blood cell gives them a high five, they feel better and they can go back to skipping.

Every two to three minutes, I stop the music and choose two more pathogens to add to the "pathogen army" but keep the same two students as the white blood cells. I ask questions such as

- Now that we have added more pathogens, do you think more of you or less of you will probably get sick?
- With more of you getting sick, and having only two white blood cells, do you think you will most likely have to wait a shorter or longer time to feel better?

I use their answers to these questions to provide clarity for them about the roles of the pathogens and white blood cells.

Effectiveness. The students learn *physically* that pathogens are disease-causing agents and that white blood cells fight off the germs to make us feel better. Since the concept is reinforced through movement with their bodies, comprehension of the subject is at a greater rate. Also, when students hear the song "Stayin' Alive," they associate the song with pathogen attack and they can easily recall the information they learned—and do well on the test—merely by playing the game.

DEBRIEF OF LESSON 5

As kids, we all learned many physically active games that as teachers we can adapt to bring topics to life through the use of movement (Baumgarten, 2006). In this situation, it was Freeze Tag. Consider other classic kid games, such as Hide-and-Seek, Simon Says, Charades, Red Rover, King of the Hill, or other forms of tag. Could you use any of these to teach your subject? Actually most of these games have, at one time or another, been adapted successfully to teaching content. Even in the first demonstration lesson, the teacher was using a variation of hopscotch.

As just one example of how this might work, think of the children's game of Hide-and-Seek. It might be adapted this way: Instead of passing out books, handouts, or other classroom supplies, consider concealing them around the classroom. When it's time to distribute them, have students stand and help each other seek out the hidden class materials.

Games are not meant only for children, although to many older people it seems that way since we learned them when we were younger. Physical games actually engage us at many levels: mentally, socially, and emotionally (Summerford, 2000). If set up properly and conducted with care, these physically engaging activities can greatly enhance learning—regardless of the age of the students.

This idea of connecting information with action—and thereby gaining the benefit of physical engagement—can be taken to even higher levels, with even more complex topics. The next lesson demonstrates how the teacher can up the ante—and the level and speed of learning—by linking the motions even more directly to the information.

LESSON 6

Using movement to verify engagement and understanding of content

Topic	Biology: The Casparian Strip
Students	High school AP Biology: ages 14–18
Primary Green Light strategy	Movement
Related strategies	Drama, novelty, and memory
Submitted by	Katie Sloan, Biology and German Teacher
	Bishop Kelley High School
	Tulsa, Oklahoma

Red Light. Previously, to explain the function and location of the Casparian strip, I primarily used lecture. To further aid students' understanding, I also showed PowerPoint slides, and together we performed labs with prepared microscope slides. Students subsequently drew and labeled the parts of the root of a plant. I also attempted to draw pictures to show the movement of substances through cells bound by the Casparian strip. None of it worked, and eventually we moved on, many students not having understood the concept.

Green Light. Now I arrange several students in a circle to represent the endodermis in the root of a plant. These are the cells that are bound on four sides by the Casparian strip. Students stand with their arms and legs spread out (so that their body is in the shape of an X) and touching the adjacent student in the circle foot to foot and hand to hand. The open spaces created by the students represent the path *through* the endodermal cells.

I then arrange another—larger—group of students outside the first group. These students represent the cortex and/or the epidermis. These students stand relatively close together, but not packed tightly. Finally, other students stand outside these two circles of students, and I explain that they represent water and minerals being taken up by the root and passing between the cells of the cortex. When the water and minerals encounter the endodermal cells, they must step through the spaces created by the bound students to reach the vascular cylinder.

Effectiveness. Simply stated, this was the most effective way I've ever presented this information. For years I attempted to explain it the Red Light way, and most of my students could never actually comprehend how the Casparian strip functioned. When I taught it using the Green Light approach explained above, they understood it in a matter of minutes.

DEBRIEF OF LESSON 6

The structure of this lesson offers the learners and the teacher several important benefits. To participate in the lesson, students obviously must be out of their chairs, a beneficial situation discussed in all the previous lessons in this chapter. In addition, however, these students' movements *match* the content they are learning. This not only accelerates and strongly embeds learning, it also offers the teacher a unique device to *assess student learning*, on two distinct levels.

First, it allows the teacher to assess student engagement. Most high school students have mastered the skill of sitting still, staring forward, and *pretending* to be engaged in a lesson—the "deer-in-the-headlights" look. They gaze with apparent rapt attention as the teacher talks, yet they are often a million miles away, daydreaming about the coming weekend, a future date, or summer. However, in a lesson like this, they have no choice but to show—literally physically demonstrate—their level of engagement.

Second, because their actions match the content, students demonstrate their level of *understanding* of the content while participating. Thus, the teacher can visually verify the level of student comprehension. In this lesson, the teacher could ask: Are they walking to the right location? Are all the parts moving at the right time? Can all students successfully play all the roles? If the answer is yes, the teacher can be confident that all the students understand the content.

You can see this concept at work in the multiplying binomials idea introduced in the debrief of the second lesson of this chapter. Again, this lesson allows the teacher to instantly assess all students' levels of engagement in the lesson and their understanding of the material. What a perfect teaching device!

Movement Is Fundamental to Effective Learning

Green Light classrooms are dynamic, lively, and fascinating places to visit! To make them so, Green Light teachers exchange "Chalk and Talk" for "Move and Improve."

They find appropriate moments to get students standing up and physically engaged in the lesson. They harness the natural desire to occasionally move and stretch, to wake up students' minds and engage them with the lesson at a higher level than if they were seated all the time. As a result, they also reduce classroom management issues, since students are no longer bored or restless.

Moreover, incorporating movement can actually improve a student's *attitude*. Consider a high school student who has five hour-long classes every day, five days a week, for an entire school year. Isn't it easy to see how some students walk into a classroom and the simple act of *seeing* the chairs strikes a note of rebellion before the class has even begun? Unconsciously, the situation has triggered a negative emotional response, which, as discussed in Chapter 7, will hamper the learning process. But imagine the difference in students' attitudes once they realize they don't have to sit still for the whole hour: that they'll be given the freedom to move; that their comfort is being taken into account. Wouldn't that make a difference?

We simply can't require our students to remain seated for extended periods of time and expect them to learn effectively. In recognition of this, Green Light teachers are leading the "movement revolution": finding ways to engage students physically with the lesson as much as possible, as often as possible, as frequently as possible.

Some educators (Red Light, anyone?) might say that this type of teaching should only be done in the gymnasium, during PE class. For many educators, there is some odd separation between the physicality of learning in the gym and the type of learning that is appropriate in the classroom. They believe that classroom learning should happen in a neat, orderly manner, fearing that movement will lead to chaos. Yet the simple truth is that real learning is an *inherently messy affair*. As students engage physically in the learning process, desks and tables will occasionally be bumped about—and this is perfectly OK! Perhaps occasional chaos could even be viewed by the teacher as necessary and important visual evidence that students are truly engaged in the learning process.

Why can't we involve students physically in all classes, whether or not the subject carries the designation "physical"? There has been a great deal of discussion in the past few decades concerning how we can teach "across disciplines"—for example, math classes teaching English as a part

of their lessons, history classes teaching science, or literature classes teaching biology. Here is a perfect place for this cross-disciplinary approach to begin. In almost any class, at any age level, we can and should include elements of physical education to achieve multiple objectives simultaneously.

For Green Light teachers, movement and physical engagement are a natural and fundamental part of the learning process. You'll notice in all chapters throughout this book how many of the demonstration lessons incorporate movement as a secondary strategy. As soon as you step away from the locked-in, traditional methods of instruction, movement immediately comes to mind as an easier—and dramatically more effective—means of teaching the same concept.

The result will be engaged, attentive students, better subject matter recall, fewer classroom management issues, and the eradication of that dreadful condition: "numb bum"!

KEY POINTS

- Students usually need permission to make themselves physically comfortable.
- Administrative activities are a great place to include movement.
- Even content with no apparent natural movement can become physical.
- Teachers need to find or create reasons for students to be out of their chairs.
- Games can become great teaching methodologies.
- Movement can allow the teacher to observe students' engagement in the lesson.
- Movement can allow the teacher to observe students' understanding of material.
- Movement creates blood flow, which brings oxygen to the brain.
- Physicality can be brought into almost every learning process.

QUESTIONS TO ASK YOURSELF

- At what level are you currently using movement in your classroom?
- Are you willing to add more physical engagement?
- Be specific: *where* will you add more movement?

5 Novelty

Novelty intrigues the mind and fires curiosity.

Does this happen in your classroom? Students arrive in anticipation of being intrigued and surprised. New subjects are introduced in novel ways. Teaching methods are innovative and creative. Even assessment techniques may be out of the ordinary. Novelty becomes a standard tool for raising students' level of engagement. The *unusual* becomes the *usual*.

NOVELTY: AN OVERVIEW

When something is *novel*—new, different, or unusual—it stands out compared to what we've experienced previously or what we're expecting currently. That which is special or unique fascinates us, makes us curious, and draws our full attention toward it. If it is novel, we are captivated.

We remember novel moments over mundane events. Think to yourself: Over the past five years, what memories stand out to you? In almost all cases, there is *something* remarkable about them. Perhaps it was a highly emotional event. Perhaps you tried something new, or visited a new place. Perhaps it was an important event involving someone you loved. Most likely there is something that was striking, unusual, or special about that memory.

Green Light teachers can enthrall their students and help them to remember the lesson by consciously including novelty in their lessons—moments that are extraordinary, atypical, or bizarre. Do something abnormal, strange, or unexpected and students will react by sitting up and paying close attention. With their attention levels elevated, students will be more likely to engage in the lesson at a higher level, process the information more deeply, and consequently remember the information better.

To Red Light teachers, the idea of occasionally using novelty may appear a bit trite: how could something so small have any noteworthy effect on the way students understand or recall new material? Green Light teachers know that many things that *seem* like simple teaching devices actually trigger a significant reaction in their students' minds. Novelty creates a critical shift in focus, setting students up for success and drawing them into the lesson.

The most significant aspect of this shift in focus is that it involves a student's *conscious* attention. The result is that outside events—which might otherwise be distracting—fade into the background as the student's focus zooms in on this new and interesting thing. Without external distractions, students are free to concentrate on and engage in the lesson.

Teachers sometimes fantasize about students walking into their classroom and saying,

I'm so glad to be here today, I can't wait to learn! I got up early and got some exercise so my mind and body could be fully ready to engage in today's lesson. I've eaten a healthy breakfast. I've reviewed everything we've done so far, to provide a solid foundation for the new information you'll be offering us today. I'm here early to get a good seat. I'm ready . . . TEACH ME!

While a few students actually do have this attitude toward learning, they are a very rare breed. More typically, students in our current educational system—especially those in middle and higher grades—are often jaded and cynical. They believe, frequently correctly, that there's nothing new to be found in the classroom. For many of them, the very act of entering a standard, ordinary, Red Light classroom triggers a state of mental distraction. They think about their girlfriend or boyfriend, Friday night's big game, or what they have planned for the coming weekend—*anything* but what the upcoming class might hold in store for them.

While Red Light teachers might believe this is not their problem and that students should simply learn to pay attention, Green Light teachers share the responsibility for keeping students focused. By including novel elements in their instruction, Green Light teachers both stop students from becoming distracted and make lessons more memorable, two important steps in maximizing learning.

We have a wide spectrum of opportunities to include novelty in the learning process. On one side of the continuum, novelty might simply be a twist to a format of instruction students have encountered previously. At the opposite end, it might be something the students have literally never seen or experienced before. The following lessons include ideas taken from many different points across this spectrum, starting with a bit of mystery.

LESSON 1

Using novelty to introduce a lesson

Topic	Joints
Students	Fifth Grade: ages 10–11
Primary Green Light strategy	Novelty
Related strategies	Movement, memory, and connections
Submitted by	Tiffany Reindl, Fifth- and Sixth-Grade Teacher
	Jefferson School for the Arts
	Stevens Point, Wisconsin

Red Light. A standard approach to this lesson would be to read about each joint in the science textbook and use the knowledge to fill in a worksheet.

Green Light. When the lesson begins, I give a hinged box to a student to "hold for me." Every now and then, I add suspense by inquiring about the box's "behavior." I arouse everyone's curiosity by occasionally asking questions like, "It's not moving, is it?" or "Is it being too noisy for you?"

When I'm ready to begin the lesson, I take the box to the front of the room and prepare my students to view the contents by saying, "Ladies and gentlemen, in this box I have an item similar to one you have in your body. It can't be the one you have in your body because I didn't get permission from your parents to dissect you, so I came as close as I could. When I hold it up, talk to your partner and see if you can narrow down where this item might be found in a human." I ask for a drum roll and the students tap on their desk with two fingers. The lid is opened on its hinge and—Voila!—I show them an actual elbow joint.

After a brief discussion about a hinge joint and its function, I direct them to complete a few physical tasks without moving their hinge joints. Sitting, eating, and buttoning a shirt become nearly impossible, and definitely very humorous. With their new awareness of joints I ask them to make a list of places in their bodies that can move and bend. After that inventory is complete, I ask them to sort their answers by common movements. Now that they have discovered all of the joints on their own, I can provide the proper science labels for the different groups of joints.

Effectiveness. Building novelty by using the closed box is a great attention getter. The use of humor with my "dissection" comment keeps the learning environment fun. Letting students activate their previous knowledge about body parts before receiving the new information is unique, playful, and very memorable to them, because it's so weird. They are all engaged in this lesson—and always do very well on the test!

DEBRIEF OF LESSON 1

This lesson on joints could have begun with the teacher simply holding one up for everyone to see. An even less interesting way to start might have been to hold up a picture and ask, "Can you all see this?" However, the ideas of

1. placing it in a box,

2. handing it to a student, and

3. building the suspense

all serve to make the introduction considerably more exciting and dynamic for the students. *Introducing* a lesson in a novel way creates a perfect platform from which to launch into the lesson, as students are now highly engaged.

In this example, excitement has been generated as students encounter a *secret* that will soon be revealed. Creating a sense of mystery can be a wonderful means of getting attention. Students in this lesson now want to know, "What's in the box?" A puzzle has been introduced into the classroom, and students now are focused on finding the solution . . . somewhere in the box. In fact, the idea of closed boxes, with their natural connection to opening presents, can be used in a variety of ways to create novelty, as this next lesson shows.

LESSON 2

Using novelty throughout the lesson

Topic	Alaskan Animals
Students	First Grade: ages 6–7
Primary Green Light strategy	Novelty
Related strategies	Emotion, movement, and socialization
Submitted by	Kristine Sobbe, First- and Second-Grade Teacher
	Goose Bay Elementary School
	Wasilla, Alaska

Red Light. Traditionally, teachers hand out packets that show the different animals that live in Alaska. They talk about the characteristics of that animal, the animal's main location, what they eat, and their habitat. The teacher then hands out papers to color and attempts to connect the students' everyday life with those animals. The lesson ends with students taking the papers home.

Green Light. In my class, students are introduced to Alaskan animals by touch, smell, and sight. In our classroom, we have a "guess box" with a hole in the top placed in the middle of the room. Students put their hands in the hole to touch what is in the box. They then go over to their desks, where they illustrate what they have felt. After each student has had a chance to touch the item in the guess box, it is revealed. From moose hide to bear hide, from caribou antlers to bear claws, students get a chance to feel almost every part of a real Alaskan animal.

We then take the idea of the guess box one step further, and they have the chance to experience what those animals eat by touch, like bark that a moose would eat; or smell, like the fish a bear would eat. They understand the full animal by sight, smell, touch, and hearing. With these senses, they start to understand how the animals are different and how they are the same. We also use math with our novelty item, like weighing or measuring a 64-inch set of moose antlers, which weighs more and is longer than most of the students.

As a class, we create our own Alaskan animal museum in our classroom with all the antlers, horns, and hides from all the animals. We then invite our parents in for a parent night to experience what we have learned. This is a chance for the students to teach a lot of the parents about Alaskan animals and share their knowledge about the areas in which the animals live. The students teach their parents how an animal feels, how to tell what it eats, and where it lives by its characteristics.

Effectiveness. At this age level, there is a wide variety in reading ability. Sometimes this disparity interferes with how well they learn. However, this is a great way to teach students of *all* reading abilities. By using the guess box, students who struggle with reading are at an equal level with those who are fluent readers. Since students are learning by *exploring*, not a lot of reading is necessary when this topic is taught in this novel and unique way. When I teach the lesson using this much novelty, all students learn—and remember—the information quickly and easily.

DEBRIEF OF LESSON 2

Again, a box has been used to teach in a novel way, although in this situation it is an *ongoing* part of the lesson, so the novelty aspect of the lesson maintains its powerful influence much longer than if it were only used to introduce a subject. Many permutations—across many subjects—are possible using this simple idea of a guess box. Students of all ages are intrigued by having to guess about something they can feel but cannot see.

Using tactile sensations to trigger learning is not something Red Light teachers would consider, which is why this approach falls into the realm of "novel" teaching. However, *touch* is very much a part of the way we learn—in fact, as infants, it's our most profound learning sense. Just because we develop other methods of learning doesn't make our experience of touch any less profound.

Our education systems should reflect the way we learn in the regular part of our lives outside school. Thus, Green Light teachers can create novelty by examining what the real world has to offer that teaching has not yet fully embraced, and finding ways to include it. When the structure of a lesson is based on a foundation of things that are real and tangible to students, they are more fully engaged, and usually learn quickly and easily (Lin, Chen, & Dwyer, 2006). When the tangible turns out to be surprising, the effect is even more memorable. . . .

LESSON 3

Using the element of surprise to capture and maintain student attention

Topic   Observation Versus Inference
Students   High school: ages 14–18
Primary Green Light strategy   Novelty
Related strategies   Socialization, emotion, and visuals
Submitted by   Rob Jensen, Earth Science and Biology Teacher
                               Hellgate High School
                               Missoula, Montana

Red Light. When presenting the difference between the terms *observation* and *inference*, Red Light teachers simply define them and move on. Those who are more adventurous illustrate the differences using examples and drawings. Green Light teachers have the kids talking all the way down the hallway after class.

Green Light. I call this lesson "The Potato Candle." A potato core with a briefly burned "wick" of slivered almond easily passes as a candle when placed in a candle holder. Without telling them what it really is, I tell the students I want to see "how good a scientist" they are and ask them to make observations of the object as I walk around the room with it. I briefly light it for more drama. We then gather their observations and write them on the board. They typically list things like "candle," "wax," "wick," and "old."

Then, quite dramatically, I light it and . . . take a big bite out of it! They are totally shocked! We now review their comments and point out how they've confused *observations* with *inferences*. My main point for the students is how their minds will fool them if they allow it.*

Effectiveness. This is timed so it's the last activity of the day and students really do talk about it all the way down the hall. Since they're talking about it, they're remembering it! The next day, we review with examples and drawings, and *not one student misses the difference between these two definitions on the exam!*

DEBRIEF OF LESSON 3

The novelty in this lesson occurs when something happens that wasn't expected. When the teacher suddenly bites into the "candle," students are startled, intrigued, and drawn in. Lessons that take sudden turns are wonderful for sparking student interest, igniting the flame of curiosity in their minds.

---

*Rob uses an apple corer found in any supermarket to core the potatoes. He advises teachers to keep the potato core wet until just prior to the lesson.

Green Light teachers actively seek the possibilities for *surprise* in their material. Of course, much like opening a real present, surprises can be good—or bad! The key here is to find good surprises, especially ones that teach. In this lesson, the surprise *extends the students' understanding of the material*, which is an especially useful application of this idea.

One additional benefit can be reaped by teachers who occasionally use surprise moments in the classroom. Students now know that their teacher likes to occasionally use the element of surprise, yet they never know when the next one might be coming. This uncertainty maintains their levels of interest for a surprisingly long time (Wolfolk, 2004).

In each of the demonstration lessons so far, novelty has been included using just one device. While this is perfectly fine, in some situations we can include novelty in multiple forms. Including more than one novelty factor in a lesson can make even a tedious topic seem exciting, as this next lesson shows.

LESSON 4

Using multiple methods of novelty within a single lesson

Topic	Layers of the Earth
Students	Fifth Grade: ages 10–11
Primary Green Light strategy	Novelty
Related strategies	Connections, memory, and visuals
Submitted by	Emma Jeter, Fifth-Grade Teacher
	Christopher Farms Elementary School
	Virginia Beach, Virginia

Red Light. Traditionally, students have a hard time with this idea because they are not developmentally ready for it. In the past, I have talked with them about the layers of the earth, and we have read about it in a textbook. Then they come up with their own labeled diagram of the layers of the earth. Just by doing that, the students are expected to learn the different layers in readiness for the test! It doesn't work.

Green Light. At the start, I don't tell the students what we are about to learn. My classroom smells of hard-boiled eggs—which is similar to gas/farts—as they walk in, so immediately I have their attention! I hand one egg to each person and they also collect a piece of paper. They divide the piece of paper into a grid containing two columns and five rows.

Next, I ask them to draw a simple diagram of their egg on the left-hand side of the paper, in the first row. Everyone now stands up and throws their egg to another person across the room. Invariably the eggs are dropped. I make sure to get in the way

Figure 5.1   Egg Chart

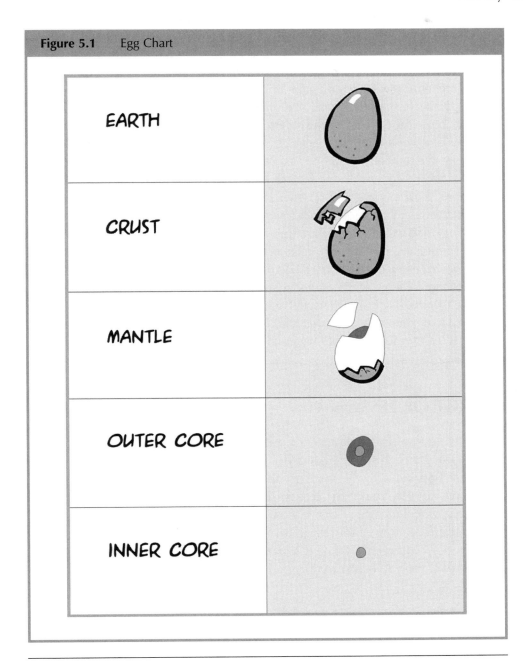

Source: Emma Jeter, Christopher Farms Elementary, Virginia Beach, Virginia.

so that *all* eggs are dropped and cracked. They love this part of the lesson! Students now draw a new diagram of their egg in the next row, making sure to include all the cracks.

Now students can break open their egg. They can use a knife or their fingers. They like to use their fingers because it's nice and messy. They draw the new diagrams of their egg in the next three rows of their grids, and then we put our eggs to one side.

The students now have a diagram of the layers of the earth. Next to the original diagram, we write the title "Earth." On that diagram of the egg, students draw what the earth looks like. On each of the others, we add the labels *crust, mantle, outer core,* and *inner core.* For a final bit of novelty, in the last part of the lesson, students write about how to eat a boiled egg from the outside into the middle. Once they are done, they take out the egg words and replace them with earth words, and we rename the instructions "How to Eat a Boiled Earth."

Effectiveness. I have found that there are two main reasons my students remember this lesson so well. First, they love to talk about bad smells. I don't know what it is about fifth graders, but anything related to a fart smell is funny. Every one of them has had an experience with a boiled egg before, so there is no fear in this lesson. They love throwing the eggs across the room and hearing them crack on the floor. Second, they love to write silly instructions and read them aloud to the class. Prior to teaching this way, I had students tell me that they found this to be one of the hardest units of science. After, they told me that they loved it, because it was so easy and fun to learn!

DEBRIEF OF LESSON 4

There are several novel aspects of this lesson. Using boiled eggs as a teaching device, tossing the eggs and deliberately dropping them, and writing silly instructions are all novel in their own ways. These three different angles on novelty make the lesson lively, keeping students engaged, participating, and learning. Sometimes, using *multiple layers of novelty* can be the most effective way to design and present a dynamic lesson that maintains student interest. This next lesson varies this approach slightly, taking just *one* of these ideas but making it an integral part of the entire lesson.

LESSON 5

The use of novel teaching props

Topic	"That Was Easy" Review
Students	Fourth Grade or higher: ages 9+
Primary Green Light strategy	Novelty

Related strategies   Socialization, tone, and movement
Submitted by   Kim Cooke, PE and Health Teacher
                                      Union County Schools
                                      Monroe, North Carolina

Red Light. Traditionally, the teacher gives review sheets on concepts or terms that will be on the test or quiz the following day.

Green Light. Students are placed in groups of three or four and are given a plastic bag of trivia questions, as well as a "That Was Easy" button, which can be purchased at certain office supply stores. Students then take turns reading the trivia questions to the other groups. The first group to hit the "That Was Easy" button and correctly answer the question receives a point. That group gets to keep the trivia question slip to help keep track of the points they have earned.

Effectiveness. This novel strategy creates high levels of student engagement. They love the opportunity to socialize in their team clusters and work together to answer all the trivia questions. Questions that are difficult can be placed at the side of the table to allow the teacher to help students understand them.

DEBRIEF OF LESSON 5

The novel aspect of this lesson is the use of an unusual teaching prop. In this type of review activity, a Red Light teacher might use the standard "Raise your hand when you're ready" technique. However, this Green Light teacher wants students to have a unique method of signaling that they are ready to provide an answer to the current question. In this case, the teacher used a "That Was Easy" button; however, this is just one possible choice to achieve the desired result. The teacher could have given each group a bell to ring, a chime to sound, or maybe—for the bravest of teachers only—a judge's gavel to pound on their desk! What student wouldn't be absolutely delighted to pound away on their desk with a gavel?

The use of creative teaching props (in Lesson 4 it was the hard-boiled egg) can be extremely effective for maintaining student interest, even when the item being used is something very simple. The key distinctions lie in how, when, and where they are used. In the next lesson, the teaching prop being used—and especially *how* it is used—takes this idea to a new level.

LESSON 6

Using the student's body as the novel teaching prop

Topic	Biology: The Human Nervous System
Students	High school: ages 14–18
Primary Green Light strategy	Novelty
Related strategies	Connections and emotion
Submitted by	Katie Sloan, Biology and German Teacher
	Bishop Kelley High School
	Tulsa, Oklahoma

Red Light. "OK. Today we're going to talk about the nervous system and how it works." Can you hear the "ughs"?

Green Light. I ask for a volunteer, making sure it's someone who isn't easily embarrassed. The student closes his or her eyes and holds out one hand. I place a coin in the student's hand and allow the student to manipulate the coin to identify it. I do this about three times using a different coin each time. The student is almost always able to identify the coin, and can also explain how it was identified—by its size, edge ridges, and so forth.

Next, I have the student lie down and lift up his or her shirt to expose a small portion of the belly. The student again closes his or her eyes. I place a coin on the student's belly and ask him or her to identify the coin, and if the student answers correctly, I ask for an explanation. The student is correct part of the time because a quarter is heavier than dimes and pennies. If I'm very careful about *placing* the coins, not letting them fall onto the student's belly, it is quite difficult to distinguish. Again, I do this about three times.

The last time, however, I replace the coin with a *drop of room temperature water* and ask for coin identification. Amazingly, the student is never able to identify it as a drop of water, and tries very hard to figure out which coin it is. This leads into a great discussion of the types of sensory neurons in our skin and how the brain processes information. The students then want to know how the nervous system works, and if they want to know, they'll learn.

Effectiveness. I have been doing this for years in all levels of science, and no one has *ever* identified the water. I've even messed up and accidentally dropped two separate drops of water on the exposed belly. The student thought it was two pennies. This unique method of giving them an introduction to the human nervous system triggers their desire to know more about how it works. In this mind-set, they are ready to learn at a high level, and I have them fully engaged in the topic.

DEBRIEF OF LESSON 6

In this situation, the novel teaching prop is the student's body! It's easy to see how this approach would capture the attention of the entire class, as the teacher begins the demonstration—and especially when a student lies on a table and exposes his or her belly! Of course, using someone's body in a public setting must be done carefully, with appropriate attention focused on keeping them both physically and emotionally safe. However, if handled with care, it can be a terrific and highly memorable way to teach.

How else could a Green Light teacher incorporate the students' whole body—or specific body parts—into a lesson? Could they use their legs, arms, feet, fingers, hands, or the tops of their heads? As an example, if learning about measurements, young students might measure various objects in the classroom by how many "hands" it is, or how many "arm lengths" it is, to teach the basic concept of units. Or, perhaps students could practice writing their spelling words in the air with their elbows, or their bottoms!

Incorporating parts of the students' bodies as a part of the lesson is especially effective because they are so intimately connected with that particular "prop." It's something they know very well. Using things that are well known to students, but not necessarily connected to the classroom, works because the *connection* is novel. One thing most students know very well is television. . . .

LESSON 7

Creating novelty through the use of well-known TV game shows

Topic	Spelling: "Deal or No Deal Grammar"
Students	Second and Third Grades: ages 7–9
Primary Green Light strategy	Novelty
Related strategies	Movement, emotion, tone, and drama
Submitted by	Sheryl Fainges, Year 2 Teacher
	Manly West State School
	Manly West, Queensland, Australia

Red Light. Traditionally, grammar is taught using a variety of techniques such as flash cards, writing on the board, or worksheets. These activities are frequently used with young students to help them identify the difference between a number, a word, and a sentence.

Green Light. "Deal or No Deal Grammar" is based on the television game show *Deal or No Deal*. Manila folders are used. Each folder contains a sheet of paper with a number, a word, or a simple sentence written on it. (I use a light-colored marker so students can't see the word, number, or sentence through the closed manila folder.) The teacher explains the rules of the game:

> No peeking at the manila folder. One student is selected as the contestant, and everyone else receives a manila folder. The contestant decides the numerical value given to each category; for example, a word = 5 points, a number = 10 points, and a sentence = 15 points. The points are added, and when the contestant reaches 30 points, he or she has the choice of choosing a small prize, such as a sticker, or continuing the game. The contestant is asked the same question as on the TV show: "Do you want the deal or no deal?"

At different intervals, the selection of prizes increases in value, for example, a small book, a voucher for a candy store, a simple game board. The aim is to reach the maximum number before selecting the manila folder with three asterisks. Three manila folders have asterisks ranging from one to three. The card with one asterisk deducts 10 points from the total, the card with two asterisks deducts 20 points, and the card with three asterisks means the game is over.

Effectiveness. This strategy has been great for involving all students, especially those who are frequently disengaged. It is also an effective method for identifying a number, a word, and a sentence. This game has been enjoyed by every grade level I have taught and is often requested by other students who have heard about it. I have several variations that I use when I work with upper grades; however, the game stays essentially the same—and is just as effective!

DEBRIEF OF LESSON 7

Successful TV shows are based on a few simple rules or guidelines. They are often successful *because* they are easy enough for both the studio *and* the television audience to quickly figure out. Consider the complexity— or lack thereof—of game shows such as *Let's Make a Deal, Jeopardy, Family Feud, Who Wants to Be a Millionaire?*, or *Wheel of Fortune*. Upon close examination, their underlying structure is quite basic.

Green Light teachers often adapt the format of popular, current game shows to support instruction, review, or even assessment of their subject. Students of all ages enjoy the novelty of being one of the participants, or playing any role in the game. In addition, because the show is *familiar* to them, most students will feel comfortable at being involved in the game—in fact, many will *volunteer* to be one of the primary players. Thus, their familiarity with the game provides them with a level of comfort, while the novelty of being *in* a game show dramatically raises their level of engagement with the material—increasing their understanding of the content.

We could take this to another level by asking students to create the questions and answers. By involving the students in developing the game's content, the lesson provides for two separate and distinct times for learning—when creating it, and when playing it—thereby doubling the amount of time they are exposed to, and engaged with, the information. This technique doubles the opportunities students have to learn the content in a novel and interesting way.

Another type of activity with which many students are familiar can be easily adapted into a novel teaching strategy: sporting events!

LESSON 8

Creating novelty through the use of well-known sporting events

Topic	"Boston Marathon" Math Review
Students	Fourth Grade: ages 9–10
Primary Green Light strategy	Novelty
Related strategies	Movement, socialization, and emotion
Submitted by	Jenn Currie, Fourth-Grade Teacher
	Commodore Perry School
	Hadley, Pennsylvania

Red Light. Traditionally, students would be instructed to complete a page from their math books as way of reviewing the most recent chapter. When complete, the class would correct it orally, and possibly hand it in for the teacher to look over. The next day would be the test.

Green Light. Students are continually asked to review and practice all types of math problems throughout the year. In this scenario, they are combining their knowledge of the Boston Marathon with real math problems. Before the race begins, a large banner running the length of one wall is hung, showing the course and "water stops." The students each receive a paper sneaker that they will move along the course map as they progress through the water stops. Placed around the room are folders—one at each water stop location—containing a mystery math problem.

Students are paired up, and each pair is instructed to stop at every water stop and solve that particular water stop problem. Upon completion of each problem, they get their answer checked by the teacher. If it is correct, they may move their running shoe to the next water stop and continue on. Pairs may hit the water stops in any order except the final one, which I playfully refer to as "Heartbreak Hill." It is the most challenging one, and to win/complete the Boston Marathon, they must solve it last. Each pair is required to complete the entire race. Those who finish first are encouraged to "coach" the others to the finish line. Once all runners have completed the course, we celebrate by rewarding each and every participant with paper trophies and a glass of Gatorade!

Effectiveness. This has been a great way to tie math in with real life. It also allows students to coach each other, which always seems to help them learn quickly. The way they attack the problems and how they talk as they work out the procedures necessary to reach the proper solution tells me they are both learning and having fun at the same time. The structure of this activity is very novel to them and always elicits a huge amount of excitement as they work together to finish the race.

DEBRIEF OF LESSON 8

In this demonstration, the lesson's structure is based on a familiar sporting event. We can adapt and develop this idea of a "cooperative race" to create a number of variations that would keep students in "novelty mode" throughout the school year, whenever the race technique is employed. Novel variations of the basic race idea might include the following:

- Changing direction, and racing backward
- Changing locations, such as racing in the hallway, in the cafeteria, or outdoors
- Changing the group size, using trios or groups of four
- Posting the paper shoe on the wall, and advancing it when groups solve certain problems or answer certain questions

For a different slant on how to handle a classroom race, with a different teaching objective, see the "Romeo and Juliet Relay Race" in the "Sound" chapter of this book.

Green Light teachers consider which sporting events are familiar to, and popular with, their students and adapt them for use in the classroom. For example, suppose a school is anticipating a big basketball game against its biggest rival. Perhaps we could introduce a basketball lesson where groups of students attempt to answer the teacher's questions on small pieces of paper. If they answer a particular question correctly, they can crumble that piece of paper up into a ball and attempt to throw it into the trash can. Making a "basket" earns the group two points, and a miss earns the group one point. The first group to reach a certain number is the winner.

Green Light teachers create endless variations of the basic structures of games such as football, baseball, soccer, and tennis. Any sporting event that students are both familiar with and care passionately about can be the extra motivation they need to fully engage in the lesson.

Novelty Versus Ritual

A ritual—the opposite of novelty—is any activity or teaching mechanism students are familiar with that is frequently repeated. This chapter deliberately emphasizes and demonstrates the importance of using novelty in the classroom. However, we must remember that ritual also serves a useful—in fact, *vital*—function in many classrooms, and should be retained to sustain student comfort levels. Examples of typical classroom rituals might include the following:

- Always covering last night's homework at the start of each lesson
- Always letting students know when they have two minutes left on an exam
- Always asking students to provide a visual response to questions asked by the teacher

Rituals can be excellent classroom devices because they offer students a safe haven for their emotions, a time when they know with certainty what is expected of them. Since so much of the learning process is by its very nature a matter of exploring the unknown, having occasional touchstones of normalcy can help students feel secure.

Yet, while rituals are important, we need to use them with care. If done too often, without sufficient variation, they may be perceived as being boring. To strike a balance between ritual and novelty, we can combine the two to create the best possible effect. Here are some examples:

- Consider the classroom ritual mentioned previously where students learn a visual signal in response to a teacher's question. Once clearly established, we can sustain this ritual, while adding novelty, by changing the *way* in which students visually respond. For example, the normal mode of response might be to say, "Raise your hand if . . . ." Instead, the teacher might add novelty by saying, "Put an elbow in the air if . . ." or "Stand up if . . ." or " Wink at me if . . . " or "Nod your head if . . . ." Or perhaps the novelty comes in the form of *speaking* instead giving a visual signal, with the teacher saying, "Say 'Good Morning!' if

NOVELTY INTRIGUES THE MIND AND INSPIRES CURIOSITY

you're awake and ready to go" or "If you know the name of at least three of the Great Lakes in North America, shout out the word LAKE." In all these variations, the ritual of providing a signal to respond to the teacher's question is kept in place, while novelty keeps the mode of responding from becoming boring.

• Suppose a teacher establishes a classroom ritual in which students know they will frequently pair up and work together, completing a worksheet, exchanging ideas, or simply chatting. Perhaps this happens in four out of every five classes students are in with this teacher. They come to expect—and appreciate—this teaching device as a part of this classroom. In the beginning, as this ritual is established, no novelty is required. Eventually, however, the teacher might want to "spice things up."

• Perhaps one day the teacher adds novelty into the ritual by asking students to decide who is "A" and who is "B." Then the teacher announces that B will go first—because B stands for "before." For novelty, this will work well a few times. However, now students will be expecting B to go first. When they come to expect this, the teacher might reverse things and announce that A will go first. When switching A and B is no longer interesting, the teacher can maintain novelty by announcing that the first person will be "whoever has longer hair" or "whoever is wearing the brightest clothing." Again, this maintains the *ritual* of working with a partner while continually introducing novelty.

• In some special cases, the ritual can become the novelty itself. In one high school classroom, a teacher wanted to start each class with some sort of brief activity to engage the students, to wake them up, and to energize them. Instead of leading these activities herself, she organized the students into small groups, and each group was responsible for leading a two to three minute "engager" to start the class. While the *ritual* was having a group start every class, the *novelty* came each day by having a different group leading a new and unexpected activity.

All these examples give students the safety of the known ritual, combined with appropriate amounts of novelty. Too often, if students come to expect certain rituals, they think they know what's coming and are no longer mentally present. The novelty alerts them that this time is different and makes them pay attention. Rituals can be useful, but combining and balancing rituals and novelty make them continually memorable.

KEY POINTS

- Novelty captivates our attention and sparks our curiosity.
- Novelty helps recall—we remember things that are unique.
- Novelty reduces external distractions and focuses students' conscious attention on the current lesson.
- Introducing new topics with novelty creates a high level of student engagement.
- Maintaining novelty throughout the lesson sustains interest.
- Novelty can be included in multiple ways and forms within a single lesson.
- Unusual teaching props (like hard-boiled eggs or the students' bodies!) create novelty.
- Many popular TV game shows and sports offer novel formats for instruction.
- *Rituals* are important classroom strategies and should be used frequently; however, a balance should be maintained between *ritual* and *novelty*.

QUESTIONS TO ASK YOURSELF

- Are your students, right now, curious enough about learning new information? If not, what can you do to help them become more interested in your topic?
- Could you truthfully tell another teacher that you totally captivate the attention of your class? If not, what can you do for this to become the norm in your classroom?
- How can you create more mystery and intrigue during your lessons?
- What fascinating props, toys, or other objects are readily available in your teaching environment? How can you include them more as a part of your teaching process?
- What basic structures—from TV game shows, sporting events, or other places—are *your* students most familiar with? How can you incorporate them into your lesson designs?
- What rituals have you established in your classroom? How might you add more life to them with increasing levels of novelty?

6 Tone

Actively access the awesome audible arena.

CENTRAL CONCEPTS

and where to find real examples to fire your imagination

*How will you use them in **your** lessons?*

ADAPT . . . ADJUST . . . APPLY

Does this happen in your classroom? When talking, the teacher uses a wide range of tone, pitch, and volume. Pauses and inflection emphasize key points and highlight new concepts. Learning is often accompanied and reinforced by music. Student-created lyrics to well-known songs are deliberately used as memory strategies. Every voice is part of the learning process.

TONE: AN OVERVIEW

Red Light teachers believe students learn best when they are quiet. In some situations, this is certainly true. However, if the only audible elements of a lesson occur when the teacher speaks, students will find it hard to learn. Instead, a classroom should be like a well-populated jungle: silence should be the rare exception rather than the rule. Usually, classrooms should *roar* with life, *teem* with the excited babble of discovery, and *echo* with the passionate sounds of learning.

What does this really mean? Well, for one thing, as discussed in Chapter 8 on socialization, students should be allowed to talk too. But that is just one important arena of tone that Green Light teachers should be including in their lessons. The *audible aspects of education* encompass a much broader universe of possibilities, including

- Learning with rhymes, *at all times!*
- Writing songs about content
- Writing new lyrics to well-known songs to illuminate concepts
- Chanting the key points of a lesson
- Ringing bells, playing chimes, or banging drums
- Playing music anywhere it might bring a lesson to life
- Giving voice to written content and making it lively and loud
- Giving students a chance to snarl or holler, growl or howl, bellow or yell!

Teachers can also help by varying their vocal range. What makes listening interesting is *variation* in the tone of a voice. Students can pay attention better when teachers use their normal vocal delivery, plus . . . whispering, shouting, exaggerating, singing, humming, being silent, or emphasizing key words.

By actively using all these various tones in the classroom, we bring our teaching space to life (Chapman, 2007). After all, life beyond the confines of the classroom reverberates with a constant barrage of sound. Sometimes loud, sometimes soft, sometimes soothing, sometimes grating, sometimes light, sometimes heavy—*but always there.* As children, we perceive the world to be this way, and we grow comfortable with the cacophony of sound that pervades our existence.

This is why the "it's-so-quiet-you-can-hear-a-pin-drop" atmosphere of Red Light classrooms is not conducive to learning. Without sound, students' brains unconsciously know that something is missing. This feeling that something's lacking—something's just not right—creates an unhelpful tension. The slow drone of the teacher's words does little to fill the enormous auditory vacuum created by closing the classroom door.

Including a variety of sounds as an integral part of instruction doesn't just increase students' comfort levels; it also helps them to learn and remember content, as the following lessons show. This first lesson combines sound with a number of other Green Light strategies to make a traditionally dry subject enjoyable, compelling, and highly memorable.

LESSON 1

Using sound—coupled with movement—to teach core concepts

Topic	Rules of Divisibility
Students	Fifth Grade: ages 10–11
Primary Green Light strategy	Tone
Related strategies	Movement, memory, and novelty
Submitted by	Emma Jeter, Fifth-Grade Teacher
	Christopher Farms Elementary School
	Virginia Beach, Virginia

Red Light. Traditionally, students learn basic divisibility rules by rote memorization. Examples of divisibility rules might include a number being divisible by 2 if it ends in 2, 4, 6, 8, or 0; or a number being divisible by three if the sum of its digits is divisible by three (for example, 231 is divisible by three because 2 + 3 + 1 = 6 and 6 is divisible by 3). The most challenging divisibility rules are for 2, 3, 6, and 9. I used to give students a copy of these rules and they would practice using a worksheet. For homework, they had to memorize the rules.

Green Light. We live in a very strong military community, so we first listened to some basic army and navy cadences. We practiced running to cadences in the yard. I would yell out the cadence and the students would yell it back to me. Then I introduced a "Divisibility Rules Cadence" I had written. I introduced it as a "life-changing cadence," telling students it would make their "division life" easier! We practiced in the classroom until they learned it, and then we practiced outside running and skipping.

Divisible, divisible! We are divisible!
Divisible, divisible! We are divisible!
To find if a number is divisible by 2,
Here is what you all must do.
Look at the digit that's on the end,
2, 4, 6, 8, and 0 are your friends.
To find if a number is divisible by 3,
Here is what you look and see.
Add up the digits and what do you get?
If it's in the 3s table, then you are set.
To find if a number is divisible by 6,
For any number that is picked.
It must be divisible by 2 and 3,
Follow the rules and you will see.
To find if a number is divisible by 9,
Here is what you look and find.
Add up the digits and what do you get?
If it's in the 9s table, then you are set.

Effectiveness. I have never had students get excited about this subject before! It was hilarious to watch them learn the divisibility cadence so they could practice it at recess with each other. I shared the lesson with another fifth-grade teacher, and students from one class would try to outdo the other. When taught this way, my students easily remember these key divisibility rules. Now when I give a test, they all ace it.

DEBRIEF OF LESSON 1

Developing teaching strategies that use more auditory elements begins by understanding the following adage:

Telling isn't *teaching.*

This means that simply speaking the right words, even if you explain or clarify the content, does not necessarily ensure effective communication.

If this teacher had simply *told* her students about the divisibility rules, many may have found this information tedious and hard to remember. Without a mechanism to help remember these rules, her students may well have struggled to keep the distinctions between the strategies straight in their minds. Instead, this teacher helped them learn by introducing a simple rhyming pattern. In this lesson, they have the wonderful opportunity to shout out loud—and move their bodies—as they learn the words to the cadence. Then, to recall the rules later, they can simply say the words in their head.

Rhyming strategies might seem silly but, as this lesson shows, they are actually remarkably effective methods of instruction. By using a verbal rhyming cadence to teach mathematical concepts, this teacher has enabled her students to ace their test.

In fact, rhymes, both verbal and written, can be valuable tools at all levels of education. In some cases, as demonstrated here, the teacher will want to develop the rhyme for the students. However, allowing students to come up with their *own* rhymes to help them memorize content can be equally effective—if not superior—to using the teacher's creations. Unleashing students' creativity in the world of rhyming is a simple, yet most effective, method for helping them learn (Heywood, 2004).

Rhymes often form the basis of song lyrics. In this next lesson, the teacher combines the power of rhyming with a well-known melody to create a lesson that is energetic, boisterous, and animated.

LESSON 2

Writing new lyrics to a well-known song to teach core content

Topic	American Revolutionary War
Students	Fifth Grade: ages 10–11
Primary Green Light strategy	Tone
Related strategies	Memory, movement, drama, and novelty
Submitted by	Cindy Rickert, Fifth-Grade Teacher
	Christopher Farms Elementary School
	Virginia Beach, Virginia

Red Light. Traditionally, the curriculum calls for students to read the social studies textbook to learn about the American Revolutionary War. They read it, complete a worksheet, and take a test. Using this approach, few perform well on the test.

Green Light. I taught my students a song to the tune of "Little Drummer Boy." I wrote the majority of the lyrics, but they helped me come up with some of them:

Seven-teen seventy-six, pa rum pum pum pum
We declared in-depen-dence, pa rum pum pum pum
Stamp tax was just too much, pa rum pum pum pum

Tea taxed—we've had enough, pa rum pum pum pum, rum pum pum pum, rum pum pum pum,
  We had to win freedom, pa rum pum pum pum, Win Freedom.
  The stud George Washington, pa rum pum pum pum
  Led the army to war, pa rum pum pum pum
  Lexington and Concord, pa rum pum pum pum
  Began this bloody war, pa rum pum pum pum, rum pum pum pum, rum pum pum pum
  War for freedom, pa rum pum pum pum, For Freedom.
  Seven-teen eighty-three, pa rum pum pum pum
  We were finally free, pa rum pum pum pum
  Loser Cornwall is was found, pa rum pum pum pum
  Surrendering in Yorktown, pa rum pum pum pum, rum pum pum pum, rum pum pum pum
  We won our freedom, pa rum pum pum pum, Our Freedom.

The first part of the song is sung without music. The second part they do as a rap, and the last part of the song is put to rock music—students dance around while singing it. They performed the song for the school, to rave reviews.

Effectiveness. When I gave the American Revolutionary War test, my students were humming the song. *The average score was in the 90s.* They still remember the song and love to perform it any chance they get.

DEBRIEF OF LESSON 2

Green Light learning has a *clamor and clatter* that resonates up and down the hallways, echoes off the ceiling, and booms throughout the school building. Notice that in this lesson, students are being given total permission to burst into song—in the middle of a class period! For many students, this is a rare and wonderful opportunity for joyful self-expression, unconditional vocal engagement, and absolute involvement in the material. How different from the typical learning environment in Red Light classrooms—and how effective!

The strategy used here is very simple: take a well-known song and write new lyrics about the content. This is such a simple concept, yet in practice it can create powerful results since it contains so many "hidden" learning moments. For example, students are learning when they initially read about the topic, when they write the new lyrics, and when they perform the song.

Notice that, in this lesson, the teacher is achieving a high level of vocal participation to a content area that may not—at first glance—seem to lend itself to anything more than book work. Some topics are naturally appealing to students. Those that aren't, however, are ripe for including innovative auditory learning techniques. It can make a world of difference for both the students *and* the teacher to connect some element of sound to challenging content areas. In their efforts to survive potentially boring or difficult content, students will *eagerly grasp the proffered lifeline*. Suddenly, this topic may strike them as interesting, worth further investigation.

Even without changing the lyrics of a song, keeping it just as it is, music by itself can be a powerful teaching device, as shown in this next example.

LESSON 3

Music as a control mechanism for stopping and starting a lesson

Topic	Musical Spelling
Students	Second Grade: ages 7–8
Primary Green Light strategy	Tone
Related strategies	Movement, visuals, and novelty
Submitted by	Sheryl Fainges, Year 2 Teacher
	Manly West State School
	Manly West, Queensland, Australia

Red Light. Traditionally, spelling is taught in rote fashion, using flash cards or by writing words on the board.

Green Light. "Musical Spelling" is based on the same basic principals as the game of Musical Chairs, although with some unique twists. The spelling words for the week are written on individual cards and placed upside-down around the room on tabletops, shelving, and chairs. I always have at least five more cards than students. Students are instructed to *safely* skip, jump, and hop around the room while music is playing.

When the music stops, they choose the card nearest to them and look at it. I select a student to say the word on his or her card and then spell it. The process is repeated with several more students. Students are praised for their efforts. The music begins, the students replace cards upside-down on the surface, and they commence skipping until the music stops and the process is repeated. I also use this strategy as a way for students to *review* the week's spelling words.

An extension activity is to have students first read their card, and then hold it tight against their tummy. Students are asked to spell the word they are holding without peeking at it. Students respond by spelling the word, then looking at the card to check their accuracy. They are rewarded verbally for their effort, and the process is repeated.

Effectiveness. This strategy is great for involving all students, especially those who might normally be disengaged. They enjoy the opportunity to physically bounce around the room, the novelty of which word they will find, and the use of the music. They *love* the music! And they always do well on the subsequent spelling tests.

DEBRIEF OF LESSON 3

Music has been included in this lesson in a way that is simultaneously directive, productive, and emotive. It is directive in acting as a signal for the start of the transition, productive in quickly spurring students to the next phase of the lesson, and emotive by creating a lively, up-tempo atmosphere in the classroom. Simply by pushing a button, the teacher has instantly triggered these highly beneficial responses.

In a Red Light classroom, the idea of introducing—or, even worse, *reviewing*—spelling words often elicits grumbles, groans, and complaints. Simply including lively music between each section of the lesson makes the classroom suddenly pulsate with energy. While there are other Green Light techniques being used in this lesson—movement, novelty, and emotions—music makes these strategies work.

We can use music in numerous ways. For example, songs can become triggers, acting as *signals* for

- The start of class
- Quiet time for small group work
- Individual reading time
- Transitions
- Clean-up time
- Lining up
- Celebrations
- The end of class

As the driving force in the lives of many students, music can bring a potent and positive energy to the classroom. Green Light teachers who introduce music often find learners eagerly asking to help create this auditory aspect of their environment. If students select the music for learning, they will own the content—making them feel part of the learning process, rather than victims of it.

Teachers, of course, must carefully review the songs students offer, checking for the appropriateness of the lyrics. However, the benefits of having students offer suggestions and ideas are enormous, especially given the *diversity* and *relevance* they will bring to the library of possible musical choices (Moore, 2007).

This next lesson strikes a different note, creating a novel—and highly useful—tone for a lesson.

LESSON 4

Using vocal variety, inflection, speed, and humor to encode core concepts

Topic	Memorizing Literature Quotations
Students	High school: ages 14–18
Primary Green Light strategy	Tone
Related strategies	Movement, drama, memory, and socialization
Submitted by	Christy Sheffield, Mentor Teacher
	Great Expectations
	Ames, Oklahoma

Red Light. Enriching students' overall grasp of literature includes developing their capability to quote stanzas of poetry and Shakespearean lines verbatim. Traditional efforts to attain student mastery in this area often include the assignment, "Memorize these lines," followed by the dreaded scenario of student recitations. Class periods spent listening to lines delivered by tense classmates in wooden, halting tones do nothing to build appreciation for Shakespeare, Robert Frost, or any quotable author.

Green Light. After students have studied *Romeo and Juliet*, explored unfamiliar vocabulary in key passages, and worked through the meaning of particular lines, I ask them to study those lines. A few days later, we stage a Romeo and Juliet Relay Race. The class is divided into two teams, and the goal is to see how many lines each team can recite in a specified amount of time.

The first team gathers at the back of the room behind a masking tape floor boundary. At the "Go" signal, the first team member flings on a costume (two or three yards of fabric that each student can drape in their own creative fashion), races to the stage (a designated area at the front of the room), recites a set of lines from the study list, and races back to the starting line. Team members are free to prompt one another and cheer enthusiastically for the racers. As soon as that first team member returns and whips off his costume, the next person in line repeats the process of costuming, racing, and reciting. The race is long enough for each student to participate several times. When the first team finishes, the second team has a chance to break the first team's record.

Effectiveness. Students quickly realize they save time by reciting without prompting, so they have "gamesmanship motivation" for saying the lines unaided. The cheering and running, along with the safety net of having the option to prompt each other, dispels any nervousness that is usually a major part of students' recitations. The costume acts like a relay wand, but it also opens up a wonderful dramatic flare for students who use the cloth as a prop and a means to create their characters. The expressiveness of students' voices blooms as they speak with the energy and excitement created by the race.

DEBRIEF OF LESSON 4

This demonstration lesson proves the point that

There is no boring content, only boring ways of teaching it.

It's easy to see that if taught the traditional way, quoting literature could be the special preserve of a few select, more able students. It might well be a painful experience for everyone else as the teacher prompts get each student to speak these "weird" words aloud.

However, using this Green Light approach—incorporating movement, socialization, vocalization, and especially *general noise*—students are now spouting literature quotations left, right, and center. The lesson feels entirely different when everyone is verbally, vocally, and *vociferously* involved in the game. Students leave behind the dry land of potential awkwardness, discomfort, and embarrassment and race headfirst into the rushing waters of excitement, interaction, and vocal participation. When taught this way, all students can now do the required task: publicly reciting literary quotations.

Most importantly, students can vocally be a part of this deliberately raucous lesson *on multiple levels.* Clearly the student on the "stage" is verbally participating by reciting the required lines. In addition, other students have permission—in fact are *encouraged*—to be involved vocally through prompting, general laughter, and wild cheers of support and encouragement. The louder the better, it's all good, as each avenue of vocal expression releases students' natural enthusiasm.

Of course, the sheer volume level of the Relay Race is not appropriate for all content areas. This next lesson demonstrates a more gentle method of adding a significant auditory component to the teaching process. Yet it is equally effective in supporting learning, since it is more fitting to the nature of the lesson.

LESSON 5

Using recorded sound so students can measure and assess their own progress

Topic	Milestone Moment
Students	First Grade: ages 6–7
Primary Green Light strategy	Tone
Related strategies	Emotion, novelty, and connections
Submitted by	Sarah Hofstra, First-Grade Teacher
	The Barstow School
	Kansas City, Missouri

Red Light. Traditionally, students are assessed on reading development through comprehension tests, multiple-choice quizzes, or essay exams. Some teachers may use individual reading notes. Teachers are able to see how students are developing by using a combination of these techniques. However, none of this provides students with any insight into their own growth.

Green Light. Several times throughout the year, I meet individually with students to read. I plug a microphone into my computer and record each student reading. Often I send the recording to the student's parent that day as an e-mail attachment. The parent receives a message saying, "Hi, Mom and Dad. This is part of one of my favorite books!" Parents love to hear their own child's voice!

I save these recordings, creating an "Audio Portfolio" of each student's reading efforts throughout the year. At selected times, I sit down with each student for a "Milestone Moment." We both put on headphones and play their readings from throughout the year up until now. By hearing their *own* voices, students realize how much their reading skills have truly grown in terms of the pace of the reading as well as increased levels of diction, inflection, and emotion.

Effectiveness. When using the traditional teaching and assessment methods, my students never seemed to understand whether their reading skills were progressing. They had no *real* way to reflect on their own growth. Scores, check marks, and explanations do not make sense to students at this age. When using these Milestone Moments, there is no way to mistake the look of pride and enthusiasm on the students' faces as they listen to their own voices! They hear themselves and instantly know they are completely different readers from the beginning of the year, to the middle, and to the end. They love recording and listening!

DEBRIEF OF LESSON 5

Even Red Light teachers ask their students to read aloud. The Green Light aspect of this lesson is that the teacher is *capturing and saving their vocal efforts.* In the process, she is allowing them to understand their progress by using the most relevant and meaningful measuring stick of all—themselves!

Given the extremely broad time horizon over which different students learn to read, it's not helpful for them to compare their reading ability to that of their peers. In a peer review, it's easy for students for whom the "reading light" turns on late to feel they are falling behind or, worse, to believe they are poor readers. This lesson allows every student to accurately gauge and be proud of their reading progress, keeping their motivation high throughout the year.

This is possible because the teacher has *seized control of the auditory component of the learning process*. The lesson elegantly underscores a vital issue to consider regarding the audible universe of the classroom:

Auditory aspects of learning should not be left to chance.

Green Light teachers include sound deliberately and strategically (Miller & Schwanenflugel, 2006). They decide when music can direct, uplift, and enhance understanding. They determine when they should speak and when they should let their students vocalize. They allow the volume to build to a learning crescendo, and use the occasional moments of silence to make a point.

Contrary to popular belief, the more we introduce sound in our classrooms, the more our students will learn. Deliberately created and properly directed, noise helps students to focus on and recall information. As Green Light teachers, we need to replace the sound of pins dropping and sighs of boredom with songs of learning, chants of recall, and cries of celebration. By using sound to keep our students alert, engaged, and interested, we create a level of learning that cannot be achieved in silence.

KEY POINTS

- We no longer believe that students learn best when the classroom is quiet: there should be a balance between focused concentration and lively learning.
- *Telling* isn't necessarily *teaching*. The learning process requires more than students merely hearing words spoken by a teacher.
- Rhymes, written by the teacher or students, can bring lessons to life while creating vital memory strategies for key content.
- The teacher should especially look for places to add sound elements where the material *seems* unappealing. Students will eagerly grasp the proffered "lifeline" and have a starting point for engaging with this particular content area.
- Music can be used as a directional tool to signal the start of a class, transitions, celebrations, or the end of a class.
- Students should be invited to offer appropriate ideas for songs they'd like to hear in the classroom, giving them a higher sense of ownership.
- Students can participate vocally as a part of the learning process on multiple levels, whether talking, cheering, singing, screaming, or laughing.
- The auditory aspects of learning should *never be left to chance*. Conscious focus is required to keep students balanced and alert, ready to engage and learn.

QUESTIONS TO ASK YOURSELF

- As a teacher, do you consciously play with your own vocal delivery? If not, what more could you do in this area to make the classroom experience more audibly interesting to your students?
- What songs do your students currently enjoy? Can any of these be used with the idea of creating new lyrics to help them remember key information?
- Are you using enough music in your classroom? Are there ways you could add even more than you are now?
- Do you consciously seek to maintain a balance between rock music and jazz, general noise and quiet, and teacher and student voices?
- Can you find a moment in your teaching where it would be appropriate for students to scream, holler, and yell in excitement?
- Are you willing to unleash their voices to create a more dynamic classroom?

7 Emotions

Learning is always *emotional.*

Does this happen in your classroom? The teacher sets the emotional tone in the classroom by being enthusiastic and passionate about the topic. Students experience a full range of positive emotions as a natural part of each lesson, being frequently amused, intrigued, fascinated, and excited. All student efforts are publicly celebrated. Students and teacher alike understand and appreciate that emotions are a critical part of any successful learning endeavor.

EMOTIONS: AN OVERVIEW

Any classroom, any setting where a group of people come together to learn, is a bubbling cauldron of emotions. Teachers who believe that learning occurs in an emotional vacuum are fooling themselves. In every moment of every day, students are pulsating with emotions. While this may not be obvious from the outside in the traditional classroom, this is because most learners have developed a finely honed survival mechanism to protect themselves in Red Light classrooms. But the masklike exterior they exhibit is merely a protective cover, hiding their emotional vulnerability.

By its very nature, learning new information requires students to explore the unknown. Thus, learning can be a risky endeavor, making it easy for negative emotions to come to the fore. Green Light teachers must therefore work *consciously* to establish and maintain the emotions they wish to elicit from their students. Without conscious attention on the part of the teacher, the dark cloud of dangerous emotions can cast a long and debilitating shadow over students' efforts.

In general, classroom emotions exist in two distinct realms. On one side of the emotional spectrum lies fear—the fear of making a mistake, of embarrassment, of public failure. This is the domain of the Red Light teacher. At the other end of the spectrum lies joy—the joy of discovery, of seeking answers to stimulating challenges, and of experiencing success. While teachers can create either atmosphere in their classroom, only the second condition facilitates Green Light learning. There's a clear choice here between creating a scary, intimidating learning environment where wrong steps lead to potential embarrassment in front of one's peers, or a safe, enjoyable learning atmosphere of exploration and discovery where all steps—whether right or wrong—are deemed worthwhile endeavors.

Safety is particularly important. If we want to lead our students to the joyful end of the spectrum, our first task is to make the classroom emotionally safe for them (Qais, 2007). In the face of cynical teenagers or boisterous six year olds, teachers may feel *they're* the ones who aren't safe in the classroom! However, the classroom is a far scarier place for students, no matter what sort of act they put on. Consider the dangers lurking within the simple act of asking the teacher a question. Students might stumble on their sentence, mispronounce a word, or ask a "stupid" question. If they do these things, they know they are going to be judged by the teacher—but, more importantly to most students, *they will also be judged by their peers*. And yet asking questions is a critical part of almost any meaningful learning process. Therefore, Green Light teachers work hard to make this, and every other aspect of learning, safe for everyone in their classrooms.

They also understand that learning is often *state dependent*, meaning there is a strong connection between the intensity of our emotions during an event and our emotional state during the act of recall. The issue this raises is that, in school settings, students often study in a banal, staid manner, but the actual test is held in an at least mildly stressful environment. The two emotional states don't match. Thus, it should be no surprise that students go mentally blank during the actual test. In the classroom, it's beneficial to create mildly elevated stress levels—anticipation, excitement, curiosity, fascination—when students are learning, to more closely match their likely state while being tested.

The other advantage of eliciting these emotions is that we are more likely to remember highly emotional events. For example, shocking events remain in our memories for a long time, and highly positive affirmations and celebrations are also easy to recall. Would you recall feeding an octopus? Bungee jumping? Falling in love? Getting married? Emotions trigger our memories. By generating an appropriate emotional state for their students, Green Light teachers help them to learn more easily. Simply put,

What we learn with pleasure, we never forget.

On the broadest scale possible, our emotions are part of what makes us human. To deny this critical aspect of humanity in the classroom is to dim the light of learning—indeed, the light of life itself. The Green Light classroom should be vibrating with positive, uplifting emotions—the anticipation of learning something new, the thrill of discovery, and the celebration of success. The lessons included here demonstrate a plethora of ways to evoke appropriate emotional states in students, beginning with perhaps the most important one of all: enjoyment!

LESSON 1

Adding joy and laughter into a potentially dry subject

Topic	Social Skills: "Eyes on the Speaker"
Students	First–Fifth Grades: ages 6–11

Primary Green Light strategy | Emotion
Related strategies | Novelty, movement, and memory
Submitted by | Paul M. Jungel, Fourth-Grade Teacher
R. E. Simpson School
Phoenix, Arizona

Red Light. While we can generally agree on the need for social skills education in our public education system, getting it across to the student in a memorable way frequently becomes somewhat of a chore. At our school, we announce the "Social Skill of the Week" during morning announcements and describe what it looks like.

It's very easy to tell students that they need to watch the speaker when he or she is talking, and that students need to follow the speaker with their eyes to show that they are tracking them and paying attention. But check closely and ask: Are they really listening and following your conversation? Do they understand what the morning announcements meant even after being told what the particular skill should look like in action? It can be pure conjecture as to whether students are on the same page as the teacher.

Green Light. During one particular week, our Social Skill of the Week was entitled "Eyes on the Speaker." The class had talked about this for the past couple of days, and I was fairly confident that they knew what it meant. The question then became how to "imprint" this idea so I would *know* they had ownership of the concept. I decided to pass out a little adhesive note to each student and had everyone draw an eyeball on it—or at least what passed as an eyeball.

Then I invited the principal down just to "check up" on my class and how they were doing with the social skill she had been announcing all week. When she walked in, I said, "Our social skill of the week is keeping your 'eyes' on the speaker." Then all together the students crumpled up their adhesive note with the eye and threw it at me.

Effectiveness. When I want students to really remember something, I like to connect an enjoyable event to it, making it memorable by having it be fun for them to learn. With the principal in the classroom watching, they all had the chance to throw paper balls at their teacher, and they loved it, laughing about it for days afterward. They definitely remembered this particular Social Skill of the Week!

DEBRIEF OF LESSON 1

The emotional foundation for any Green Light classroom should be one of joyful engagement in the learning process. Too often teachers take themselves, and their content, far too seriously. Why not do the serious teaching when it is required, and then balance out the emotional tone of the room with laughter and playfulness, or at the very least a sense of light-heartedness? Why not play more often or break a bout of serious teaching by allowing the class to burst into laughter? What could possibly be wrong with students actually enjoying themselves?

Some teachers, of course, will fear that any hint of laughter and fun will result in a loss of control. However, if students are allowed to freely express themselves, they quickly learn when it is appropriate to laugh and when it is time to concentrate. It is only the too rigidly controlled classroom that shatters under the influence of student enjoyment. The teacher in this lesson obviously knows his students well, and has created a flexible atmosphere of appropriate playful engagement.

When students have experienced the release of laughter and joy in the classroom, it is easier to guide them—when appropriate—into the times of focused concentration they will certainly need. Since our bodies naturally relax down from the high of laughter into a state of calm, it's easy for teachers to move their students to a point where they are quiet, focused, and receptive to learning.

However, since many students will have experienced only Red Light classrooms in their past, it is the teacher's responsibility to lead the way in the arena of relaxed learning—as the following lesson shows quite clearly.

LESSON 2

Getting students to relax in potentially tense situations

Topic	The First Day of School: Expectations
Students	High school freshmen: ages 14–15
Primary Green Light strategy	Emotion
Related strategies	Novelty, movement, tone, and socialization
Submitted by	Karen Renaud, High School PE Teacher
	Ashland High School
	Ashland, Massachusetts

Red Light. The Red Light approach to this first day of class consists of waiting for the students to arrive at the gym; showing them where to sit; introducing myself; passing out the course expectations, policies, and syllabus; and then reviewing everything together. I would also show them where the locker room is and discuss the safety rules.

Green Light. The two other teachers from my department and I work as a team to welcome the kids and share our philosophy of learning. I stand at the gym doors and welcome each student with a handshake and a 3- × 5-inch index card that says "You're Awesome." One of my colleagues waits for the students to get to the bleachers and also welcomes them with a handshake and directs them to their "luxurious" seating area. By this time, the kids are already looking at us like we have lost our minds.

Once the kids have settled in, I start some music, usually "Wild Thing," "Welcome to the Jungle," or the theme from *The Addams Family*—something unique to set the appropriate tone. Our third colleague walks into the gym while the music is playing. He waves like he is some kind of star as we encourage the kids to applaud. He begins his speech by welcoming the kids to the "Big House" and very humorously describing the differences they will find between middle school and the "Big House." He then introduces each of us with an exaggerated list of our skills, experiences, and areas of expertise. We take turns sharing our department philosophy of "learning while having fun" and how simple it is to succeed in class. We also put a humorous spin on the "Golden One-Way Ticket" to the office used on the rare occasions that a student has some "difficulties with self-control."

We wrap up our first day by going on the "Great Journey of Exploration." We take our classes on a walk to all of the different locations inside and outside of the building where we will meet during the school year. We stop along the way to share real—and occasionally fictional—stories about these locations. We do it to help the kids relax on their first stressful day of high school, to grab their attention, to make them curious about their "crazy" teachers, to make them laugh and want to come back!

Effectiveness. Kids walk into the gym on that first day nervous and highly stressed. They rarely look happy and are expecting that they will just be bombarded by more "rules and expectations." This is not the emotional connection we want them to have with our classes! In addition, many high school students simply no longer see PE class as fun; they see it as painful. With our first meeting, we challenge all of those beliefs and feelings. By the end of class, the kids are much more relaxed, they have laughed, and they leave with smiles on their faces. Rather than being apathetic, many of them are thinking how cool the year is going to be having us as their teachers. We find that they are curious and more open to us. We open the door to learning on the first day by using positive emotions and novelty to engage our students. We started doing this a few years ago and wouldn't think of doing it any other way.

DEBRIEF OF LESSON 2

The teacher always sets the tone. If the teacher is willing and able to be occasionally playful, the students will mostly likely feel much more comfortable following his or her lead. The manner in which these teachers are starting the year helps to relax the students—making them more emotionally comfortable. The more comfortable they are in the learning environment and with their teachers, the more willing they might be to engage in lessons and to take the risks necessary to learn the material.

Some educators might question whether it is right to "waste" a whole class this way. The answer is a resounding "YES!" The key is the critical nature of the emotional tone that is being established for the students. With this as a beginning point to work from, subsequent classes have a much better chance of being successful than if the emotional atmosphere had *not* been directly addressed. In addition, it may also be important throughout the year to occasionally take more time—although perhaps not an entire class period—to consciously reestablish and reaffirm the appropriate tone of the learning environment. All too easily, given the demands of the amount of content to be covered and the various tests required, both teacher and students can drift off into a negative emotional state as the school year drags on. Doing something—anything!—to reignite the foundation of pleasant emotions will pay dividends in the long run.

Yet consciously focusing on the emotional tone of a classroom is not just about creating laughter and playfulness. While this is a critically important component to address in Green Light classrooms—especially in this present age of over-testing students—other emotions are equally important for other content areas. In this next situation, an entirely different emotional state is not only useful, but almost *demanded* by the nature of the topic being addressed.

LESSON 3

Learning through creating a thoughtful, reflective classroom atmosphere

Topic	Substance Abuse: Drinking and Driving
Students	Ninth Grade or higher: ages 14+
Primary Green Light strategy	Emotion
Related strategies	Movement, tone, and visuals
Submitted by	Kim Cooke, PE and Health Teacher
	Union County Schools
	Monroe, North Carolina

Red Light. Traditionally, the teacher lectures, usually using overheads. Students sit at their desks lined up in rows and take notes on the consequences of drinking and driving. The teacher then emphasizes the importance of making the "right choices."

Green Light. I create a five- to seven-minute slide show with pictures of victims who have died or have been grievously injured by a drunk driver.* Music—"Tears in Heaven" by Eric Clapton—plays in the background as students watch slides of people

---

*Pictures and stories concerning victims of drunk driving accidents can be obtained at www.madd.org.

of all ages who have been affected by someone who has made a wrong choice, deciding to drive after they have been drinking.

I then allow students to stand up (after they have been sitting for approximately 15–20 minutes) and have them "vote by their feet." I ask 8 to 10 questions about substance abuse. Instead of bubbling in the correct answer (A, B, C, or D or True/False), the students walk to the identified corner in the room that is labeled with either an A, B, C, or D or the True or False wall. For example, in the United States someone is grievously killed by a drunk driver every A, 45 minutes, B, 23 minutes, C, 60 minutes, or D, 90 minutes (the answer is B).

After this question sequence is complete, I have students sit down, and I get their attention by playing a heartbeat.* I read to the class the story of how one victim lost his or her life, killed by a drunk driver. I repeat this procedure every 23 minutes to reinforce the concept that in America someone is killed by a drunk driver every 23 minutes.

Students then receive a "Mystery Bucket," which contains red construction paper, markers, tape, and a list of victims who have died from a drunk driving accident. Students create a "brick wall memorial" to honor the victims by writing their names on homemade "bricks" and placing them on the hallway wall outside the classroom. This creates a visual representation for students of how many innocent victims' lives were carelessly taken by a drunk driver. In the last five minutes of class, students get out a "Ticket to Go" form from their Mystery Buckets and answer at least one of the following questions:

1. What is something you learned today?

2. Was anything unclear?

3. Write a sample question for a challenge (I call tests or quizzes "challenges").

Students hand these tickets to me as they leave the classroom.

Effectiveness. Student engagement is high! I always have tissues ready during the slide show because my students usually get very emotional when seeing real pictures of people—especially young children—who have died from a drunk driving accident. Students feel empowered to honor the victims when they are creating the brick wall memorial. Most importantly, students say they *deeply feel* the impact of realizing that they are not invincible and risky behaviors can cost them their own life, as well as someone else's.

DEBRIEF OF LESSON 3

Clearly, this is a serious topic. Students will better understand the importance of this information if the teacher establishes and maintains a deeply profound emotional tone during the lesson. Then, through thoughtful

---

*The sound of a heartbeat can be downloaded from www.itunes.com.

reflection and discussion, students are more likely to remember the critical core of the lesson. The issue is an important one for life in general, and this teacher wants students to be empowered to make good choices for themselves in the future. The most effective way to ensure this happens is to provide a potent emotional connection between the experience of the lesson and the information students need to remember long after they leave the classroom.

Green Light teachers carefully consider which emotional state might be most appropriate for teaching a particular topic. Of course, not all subjects require the level of intensity demonstrated in this lesson. However, many topics could benefit from the conscious inclusion of an emotional tone when presented to students. As just one example, consider a history class. Far too often, the subject of history is taught in a dry, uninteresting manner. And yet most memorable events in history, when they actually happened, were far from boring! The people in those situations were brimming with hopes and dreams, wants and desires, worries and fears. How can history teachers make students truly feel the agony of the slaves, the breathtaking fear of exploring the unknown wilderness, or the exhilaration of declaring independence? This is how Green Light teachers think when creating lesson plans.

With topics that have no natural emotional tone, Green Light teachers may want to consider using playfulness as their "default" emotion. Could English be taught in a playful way? Mathematics? Biology? Literature? While it may not be possible to teach *all* lessons with this type of emotional overtone, those lessons that *can* be taught using at least *some* level of emotion will spring to life for students—as this next lesson quite clearly shows.

LESSON 4

Arousing anticipation and curiosity to bring routine lessons vibrantly to life

Topic	Flash Card Drills
Students	First–Eighth Grades: ages 6–14
Primary Green Light strategy	Emotion
Related strategy	Novelty, visuals, drama, and socialization
Submitted by	Shari Rindels, First-Grade Teacher
	Catalina Ventura School
	Phoenix, Arizona

Red Light. Traditionally, to learn math facts, high-frequency words, vocabulary words and definitions, spelling words, and so forth, teachers may pair up students, give them a pack of flash cards, and tell them to practice drilling each other for "x" amount of time. Students often moan and groan because it gets old and it's boring, but still—it has to be done.

Green Light. I like to spice up this potentially dry but necessary part of school by using "Mystery Bags." Instead of just handing a pair of students the flash cards that they need to practice, I put the flash cards in gift bags. Everyone occasionally gets cool gift bags, and we hate to throw them away! Now you don't have to—just glue a question mark to the front and back of the bag and presto—it becomes a Mystery Bag!

There are many ways to use these Mystery Bags:

- Choosing—I like to place the bags around the room and have students go sit by the bag they want. Energy levels instantly rise!
- Using—I sometimes have all bags contain the same flash cards, so everyone practices one time and it's done. Or, I'll have different flash cards in different bags and allow the students to trade with each other when they finish with their starter bag. I often set a timer and let them trade bags until time is up.
- Storing—I usually let the bags remain visible on shelves, or hung on the wall, so students can use them when they finish with work, or during free choice time.

Effectiveness. Flash card drill time is not nearly as drab, dreaded, or dreary as it once was for my students. Attitudes are more positive and life is more enjoyable just because of one simple change—the packaging! I love it when students beg for three more minutes to do Mystery Bags!

DEBRIEF OF LESSON 4

This simple yet effective teaching device opens up a whole new emotional realm teachers can tap into in the classroom. Perhaps these emotions are best summed up by the wonderful word *wonder*. Students wonder what is going to happen, who will be involved, and where the lesson is heading. Wonder creates excitement, anticipation, and curiosity. It draws the learner in toward the material with little or no direct coaxing on the part of the teacher.

Green Light teachers create a feeling of "tell me more" in their students' minds. When students desire more information, are fascinated by the direction of a lesson, or are simply curious to know more about a particular subject, they are mentally and emotionally ready to learn. In the "tell me more" mind-set, students often begin to seek out the information on their own, actively searching for answers to their own questions, instead of ones posed by the teacher. By doing this, they are taking ownership of their own learning process. Ownership of the material—gaining a personal grasp on a concept—is critical to both learning information and using it in higher-order thinking, as shown in Lesson 5.

LESSON 5

Building confidence to use as a foundation for subsequent learning

Topic	Bill of Rights
Students	Fifth Grade: ages 10–11
Primary Green Light strategy	Emotion
Related strategies	Movement, tone, and memory
Submitted by	Cindy Rickert, Fifth-Grade Teacher
	Christopher Farms Elementary School
	Virginia Beach, Virginia

Red Light. Traditionally, students learn the U.S. Bill of Rights from reading the original document. Students are given a list of the first 10 amendments and are expected to read them over and learn them. They study this and take a multiple-choice test to check comprehension.

Green Light. In my classroom, we make a "Bill of Rights My Way." First, we put each amendment into modern context. As a class, we decipher the meaning of each amendment and make a Bill of Rights My Way using terms that are understandable to the students. Each amendment is described using no more than five words, and sometimes we even use slang to make it more fun.

Example: Amendment 3 deals with the unlawful quartering of soldiers in homes during any time, whether peace or war. My students came up with the idea that we could make this amendment: "No soldiers in my crib!" The word *crib* is harmless current slang for "house." I caution against using too much slang because it is not the "proper" usage, although a little here and there doesn't hurt. It also lets the students know that they can be a little silly and learn at the same time.

Once we had rewritten the Bill of Rights in our own terms, it took my students only a matter of minutes to memorize the actual Bill of Rights. They could understand what it really meant and felt connected to it. Their feeling of connection to the information, ownership of their understanding of it, made a subject that had previously been very difficult to learn a breeze.

Effectiveness. *Every student in my class made a 100 percent on the Bill of Rights test.* Not only did they memorize all the amendments, but because they knew what each one meant, they were able to apply it to higher-level-thinking questions easily. They weren't hung up on trying to remember each amendment, so they were free to focus on applying the knowledge.

DEBRIEF OF LESSON 5

Students gained significant *confidence* in this lesson when the teacher allowed sufficient time for them to process the information and make it meaningful. We have already discussed the importance of meaning in Chapter 3 on connections. This lesson is included in the current section because of the emotion—confidence—it generated in the students and the positive effect of these emotions on how students process, analyze, understand, and apply the information.

Red Light teachers would rarely consider the emotional connection students have to the subject matter, except possibly as an irritating by-product of a normal lesson—meaning that now they have to deal with something *else* in the midst of an already difficult lesson. Their only expectation of how students gain confidence is as a result of their own hard work—it has nothing to do with how the material is presented. In this case, however, the sense of confidence the students gained emerged as a direct result of the opportunity they were given to process the information. It was critical to their success, and drove them to a deeper understanding of material that had previously been challenging for them just to remember—much less understand and apply.

Internal confidence drives students to learn more (Hanze & Berger, 2007). When they succeed, they feel powerful, capable, and competent. Teachers who consistently generate that sense of confidence in their students create successful learning outcomes without a major increase in effort on their own part. And when students succeed, they are ready to celebrate!

LESSON 6

Celebrating success to create a positive attitude toward learning

Topic	Peer Praise
Students	Second–Fifth Grades: ages 7–11
Primary Green Light strategy	Emotion
Related strategies	Movement, memory, connections, and tone
Submitted by	Karoline Gebbett, Foreign Language Teacher
	Mountbatten Languages College
	Southampton, England

Red Light. Small student achievements often go unrecognized beyond a simple "yes" or "good" from the teacher. Oddly enough, students usually get a substantially larger reaction to *bad* behavior.

Green Light. In my French classes, the whole class acknowledges an individual's achievement with a dramatic verbal and physical gesture. I set this up early in the year. When a student does something successfully for the first time, I stop the class and say, "Un, deux, trois—superb!" At the same time, I stretch out my arms with my thumbs up and point my thumbs at the student in question. Then I ask all the students to repeat "superb" and repeat the gesture. Once the class catches on, all I have to do is say: "Un, deux, trois..." and all students join in. It's a very powerful moment, and the individual being praised lights up with pleasure.

Later, when we've learned other praise words, like *magnifique*, I let the students choose their own celebration word, so the process also helps to expand their vocabulary. I make sure we acknowledge individual achievements—what might not be a big deal for one student could be huge progress for another—so the technique also allows students to appreciate each other and recognize that praise isn't just for the top performers.

Effectiveness. I find this technique creates an extremely positive classroom atmosphere. Peer recognition is a powerful motivator. I had one very shy child who didn't speak for the first term. But when she finally whispered her very first French word, and the class positively rang with acknowledgment, it was a huge turning point. Now, although still very shy in English, she is happy to chat in class in French.

DEBRIEF OF LESSON 6

One of the most important—though often overlooked—methods of harnessing emotions in the classroom is *fully* celebrating student successes. Red Light teachers often take a student's success for granted, and fail to recognize the effort that individual may have expended in reaching this particular level of achievement. Student successes should be rewarded frequently, loudly, and publicly! Having success *visibly* rewarded drives all learners to work harder so they too can receive glowing praise from the teacher and their peers.

In this particular lesson, the teacher is continuing to teach the content of the class—French—while eliciting and embedding these important feelings of acknowledgment and success. Using the content to celebrate reinforces the learning while also eliciting emotional exuberance. Green Light teachers offer their students a wide variety of ways to praise the efforts of those around them, some like this lesson utilizing the content of the class, as well as others that are more general.

Celebrations offer Green Light teachers the opportunity to re-energize the class. They can be as simple as asking students to stand up, turn to each other, and say, "Well done!" "Awesome!" or "Amazing!" They can be physical, such as high-fives or handshakes. Or they could be a combination of these two strategies, as the technique shown in this lesson demonstrated.

They can be individual, where all students applaud a particular individual, or a whole group acknowledgment, where everyone celebrates the group's success in achieving a particular goal. An example of a group celebration might be when the teacher turns on a particular song and

everyone has one minute to boogie and move in celebration. Green Light teachers realize how much students enjoy these moments of celebration and release—and how hard they will work to achieve them.

Rituals for celebration are important to establish and maintain as a significant part of any successful classroom routine. Whatever form they take, in Green Light classrooms, celebrations that lock in a sense of accomplishment and a feeling of success should happen often enough that *everyone* knows they have a chance to get in on the game.

Always Up

At the risk of overgeneralizing, many classrooms are depressing. The way they are physically arranged, the way teachers handle lessons and discipline, and even the length of the class can all quickly dampen students' natural enthusiasm for learning. Thus, Green Light teachers pay careful, conscious attention to the lighter side of education. A useful phrase for this dynamic could be

Always up!

This phrase means that Green Light teachers consciously include the "up" side of learning and maintain positive emotions in the classroom.

If students get too down about an upcoming exam, find a way to bring their emotions back up. If they are feeling hesitant, worried, depressed, or frightened, they are likely to be in a poor emotional state to take a test. Help students learn to adjust their own emotions and bring themselves back up to a more resourceful state. The educational journey of most students will be filled with enough natural stumbling blocks, obstacles, and wrong turns. Green Light teachers balance this by keeping students focused on their achievements and providing them with moments of laughter, enjoyment, and fun.

Keeping the idea of "always up" alive in the classroom—and in life—can sometimes be challenging. Yet it can also be incredibly rewarding. Students in more engaging and enjoyable classrooms don't just get better results; they learn that *happiness is a choice* and that nothing *has* to be boring. What better gift to give them than the ability to *choose* to have fun—and to harness the energy that comes from enjoyment to improve their learning. Green Light teachers show their students what it means to live by the motto of "always up," in the process teaching them one of the most important lessons in life: how to be happy!

KEY POINTS

- Learning is *always, always, always* emotional.
- What we learn with pleasure, we never forget.
- The *extent* of our engagement with the learning process—and our subsequent memory of the material—often depends on our emotional *state*.
- Moments of enjoyment should not be left to chance; they should be deliberately included as a critical component of most lesson plans.
- The teacher sets the emotional tone of any classroom.
- Where possible, the emotional tone of a lesson should match the topic.
- If no natural emotional tone exists, playfulness is a good default option.
- Establishing the emotion of *wonder* works . . . wonders.
- When students are in "tell me more" mode, half the work is already done.
- Creating a feeling of confidence, a sense of accomplishment and success, drives students to learn more, *without extra effort by the teacher*!
- Success should be rewarded, loudly, publicly, and frequently.
- Always up!

QUESTIONS TO ASK YOURSELF

- Are you willing to allow students to express themselves emotionally?
- Are you willing to help set the emotional tone in your classroom?
- Are you willing to be playful, as the situation demands?
- Are you willing to specifically include emotion as a part of your lesson design?
- Are you using deliberate and conscious techniques to arouse students' emotions?
- Do you allow your students to celebrate their successes often enough?

8 Socialization

Talking students are learning students.

How will you use them in your lessons?

ADAPT . . . ADJUST . . . APPLY

Does this happen in your classroom? Lessons are designed with frequent opportunities for social interaction. Students regularly process new information through peer-to-peer conversations. Occasionally, students even become teachers. Their conversations open the doorway to improved understanding, better questions, and sharper recall.

SOCIALIZATION: AN OVERVIEW

Here's a radical idea: For teaching to be effective, students need to *talk* about what they are learning. Why? Because, to *talk* about a topic, students must first think about and mentally process the information. Then, as they talk, they are verbally processing the information. As a result, they will come to a better understanding of the new information. They will pick up and practice using its vocabulary; take a higher level of ownership for their learning; and better recognize connections between new concepts, terms, and ideas. When all these things happen, students are more likely to understand and remember the new information. It's that simple. Thus, Green Light teachers should not only allow, but actually *encourage*, students to talk to each other in the classroom (Myhill, Jones, & Hopper, 2005).

Instinctively, most teachers seem to recognize this essential component of effective instruction. However, in a traditional classroom, the primary way students are given permission to talk—often the *only* way—is by responding to a question posed by the teacher (Pontefract & Hardman, 2005). While the teacher's intentions are well-meaning, this singular avenue for verbal expression is fraught with potential problems. What if the selected student doesn't know what to say? What if the answer is wrong? What if the student stumbles on the words and feels embarrassed? Red Light classrooms—where students are only allowed to talk *publicly* in response to the teacher's questions—are high-threat learning environments. The talking that these classrooms permit is unlikely to assist the learning process.

By contrast, Green Light teachers find other ways of providing students with opportunities to talk, within the context of a lesson—many of which are demonstrated in this chapter. These alternative methods allow students to learn through social interaction.

Student-to-student interactions are not only powerful learning opportunities; they also help teachers to

Crack the lecture habit!

While lecturing can serve an important function in delivering information, it is only *part* of the much greater learning process. Lecturing is good for directly giving students key content and allowing the teacher to explain, clarify, and elaborate as needed. However, it can't go on for too long. After approximately 10 to 15 minutes of lecturing, students will experience mental overload (Ruhl, Hughes, & Schloss, 1987).

Information overload has a number of unhelpful side effects: concentration wavers, interest diminishes, and the quality of notes suffers. To prevent overload, Green Light teachers allocate "brain breaks" at frequent intervals for students to discuss the new information with their peers. This allows them to "download" the information, process it, make connections, and prepare for the next wave of input. Ultimately, it makes the learning process much more effective, as students become more resourceful learners.

A tenured professor in Sydney, Australia, recently decided to try this idea (at his request, he will remain anonymous). He is a self-proclaimed Red Light teacher. While not overly proud of this distinction, he was unsure how to change the approach he had used for years in his lectures. Finally, he decided to take what he deemed to be a huge risk, and try this "pause procedure." He reported that it was as if a magic lever had been flipped on in the students' minds. The simple addition of this one strategy switched his classroom from dull red to bright green! Learners who had previously been quiet or disengaged came blazingly to life, enjoying their newfound freedom of discussion. While he has changed little else in his teaching style, his classroom now vibrates with life.

Teachers interested in creating opportunities for social interaction have numerous techniques at their disposal. One novel way might be use an old-fashioned hourglass designed to time 15 or 20 minutes. As class begins, show the hourglass to the students and inform them, "When the sand runs out, it will be time for you to work briefly with each other." Turn over the hourglass and begin the lecture. If you don't notice when the sand runs out, your students certainly will!

Pausing in the middle of a lecture to allow students to talk to each other is only one means of bringing more social interaction into the classroom. The following lessons open the door to the endless possibilities for teachers to include the important ingredient of student-to-student conversations during lessons. This first example goes right to the heart of the matter, showing how effective this strategy can be when applied properly.

LESSON 1

Talking in small groups to process new information

Topic	Math: Order of Operations
Students	Ninth Grade: ages 14–15
Primary Green Light strategy	Socialization

Related strategies   Movement, novelty, and memory
Submitted by   Duke Kelly, Former Math Teacher
                                        Education Illustrated, LLC
                                        Howell, Michigan

Red Light. In a typical classroom, this lesson begins with the teacher announcing, "Today we're going to learn about the order of operations." Students stare blankly. The teacher explains and then demonstrates using sample problems. Students are given a handout containing countless problems and are told to work quietly at their desks.

Green Light. As the lesson begins, students are organized into groups of three or four. They are shown a series of math problems taped to the walls of the classroom. As a group, they go to one of these and see not only the problem, but also the answer. The directions are, "If that's the correct answer, *what order* would you have to do the operations in to arrive at that answer? Do you have to add first, or multiply, or do the exponent, or . . . ?" As a group, they turn back to the problem and work together to decide which order was necessary to arrive at that answer. Then they choose another problem to work on.

When they sit down, I ask them to develop some "It seemed . . ." statements, such as, "It seemed like we always did the exponent first" or "It seemed like we always had to multiply before we added." They discuss this for several minutes. Finally I ask for "It seemed . . ." statements from various groups, and use what they have developed to introduce them to the correct order of operations:

Parentheses—Exponents—Multiplication—Division—Addition—Subtraction

Effectiveness. What's amazing is that the groups often arrive at the proper sequence of operations long before I even teach it to them. Perhaps more importantly, they believe they came up with this order *on their own*. In this situation, as they work with their group, it feels like it's "their" information. Of course I follow this experience with practice problems for them to work on—first in a group where they can help each other, and then on their own. They often say this is one of the easiest concepts of the year for them to learn, and *they always do extremely well on tests* about the order of operations.*

DEBRIEF OF LESSON 1

As the teacher indicates in his "Effectiveness" section, by working together in a social situation, this lesson allows students to learn the material rapidly on their own (Fernandez-Berrocaal & Santamaria, 2006). Instead of

---

*A more detailed description of this lesson is available in the book *Calculated Success* by Duke Kelly, available at www.educationillustrated.com.

being handed more information they simply need to memorize, students *discover the core of the lesson on their own*. Thus, they take ownership of the material. This is not an isolated incident: whenever students are given a chance to work together, the odds increase that they will feel more connected to the core content, leading to a deeper understanding of the concepts and a higher level of comprehension (Williams, 2007).

However, Green Light teachers need to take care of the way they set students up to work together. This lesson incorporates peer coaching, which can be an excellent teaching strategy (Cropley, 2006). However *setting up* these peer coaching situations can create problems. Sometimes, when the groups are first organized, the general feeling is, "OK, all the smart students, please go help the dumb ones!" Of course, while it is never explicitly stated that way, the feeling is still there, and *students all know it*! Notice how in this lesson the students found their own groups and the whole lesson was handled in such a way that students were never embarrassed. The learning for Green Light teachers is that students need to support each other as equals for the technique to succeed.

This may seem a minor point; however, if teachers don't handle the setup appropriately, the resulting negative emotional tone can pervade the entire lesson, undermining any value gained by the students' interaction. Notice how, in the remaining lessons, wherever students are helping each other learn, there is never the tone of "smart versus dumb," "good versus bad," or "superior versus inferior."

Notice also how, as in this next demonstration, students gain several benefits from helping each other during a lesson.

LESSON 2

Combining multiple socialization techniques within a single lesson

Topic	Coordinate Pairs
Students	Fourth Grade: ages 10–11
Primary Green Light strategy	Socialization
Related strategies	Tone, novelty, visuals, and movement
Submitted by	Eva Matz, Academic Support Teacher
	Gregorio Esparza Elementary School
	San Antonio, Texas

Red Light. Traditionally, students are introduced to coordinate pairs by being shown a grid labeled with the *x*- and *y*-axis. Students are informed that the *x*-axis runs horizontally and the *y*-axis runs vertically. The teacher models a coordinate pair, such as (6, 4), and demonstrates the technique of following along each axis until the desired point is located. The teacher models this process several times. This is followed by independent practice on the part of each student.

Green Light. I prefer to involve students in learning about this topic. I introduce the unit by telling students where their next field trip is going to be. I pull out a map of the city and find the location, making sure to exaggerate the use of coordinates. I then explain that knowing how to use coordinates helps find the destination on the map. I make a connection for them between the grid of a map, and the grid of the x- and y-axes on a coordinate plane.

The class now moves to a huge "map"—a taped grid—on the floor. Students form groups, take turns calling out coordinate pairs off of index cards, and help team members locate their "address"—a specific point on the floor grid—by walking around the map and stopping at the proper coordinate pair. The group celebrates each time they successfully locate an address.

Once they understand the general concept, I add another layer to the lesson. This time students are in pairs. Each person stands on a point, and they tell each other where they think they are. The other person checks them for accuracy. After a few rounds, I tell them to occasionally make a *deliberate* mistake when telling their partner about their "address" and see if their partner can catch the mistake. They love this part, being deliberately wrong, and race around trying to trick the other person.

Effectiveness. I find that students remember more when they are working with each other as they learn. Getting students up and out of their seats, and having them form groups, helps heighten their level of engagement. They love to talk to each other anyway, and now they get that chance! Students open up to participating with the support of teams or a partner, and truly learn what they need to know in a fun way.

DEBRIEF OF LESSON 2

As in the first lesson, students are directly helping each other learn. However, importantly, this teacher is also providing novelty and variety. For social learning to be most effective, *students need to interact in a variety of formats* (Moura, 2006).

In the initial stage of this lesson, groups of students are helping each other understand the concept of coordinate pairs. If the learning ended here, some of the students would likely get the concept, while others might well require further clarification to truly be confident in their understanding. Given that some of them now feel they have mastered the topic, if they continued learning in the same way, some would likely get bored with the process. The teacher addresses this potential problem by providing two additional, distinct ways for them to check each other's knowledge as they continue to learn. First, they work in pairs and do "error correction" with each other, and second, they make deliberate mistakes.

This final stage of the lesson is particularly noteworthy. This approach is sometimes labeled "mismatching"—where students deliberately make mistakes and try to catch each other. The instructions normally given to pairs, or groups, are to work together to find the *correct* idea, the *approved* solution, or the *right* answer. While in most situations this is perfectly acceptable, many students love the opportunity to do something wrong, especially when it is on purpose! While students think they are merely having fun, teachers should realize that the only way they can know they are wrong is if they know what is right! Without consciously realizing it, they are cementing their understanding of the content.

This next lesson introduces another variation on a social teaching strategy.

LESSON 3

Students indirectly helping each other review and process information

Topic	Family Feud Review
Students	First Grade: ages 6–7
Primary Green Light strategy	Socialization
Secondary strategies	Novelty, tone, and memory
Submitted by	Kris Long, First-Grade Teacher
	Gulliver Academy
	Coral Gables, Florida

Red Light. Traditionally, review of concepts is done by question and answer, drill and practice, or worksheet.

Green Light. I split students into two "families." One member of each family comes to the front of the room and is asked a review question from one of many subject areas. The students tap a buzzer if they think they know the answer. If the answer is correct, their family gets three more opportunities to answer questions. As with the TV game show, if they get them all correct, they earn a point. However, I use a twist on the original game show, adding extra times for them to "huddle" with their families and discuss answers, since this is where the real learning—the actual review process—is happening!

Of course, if the first person is incorrect, the second person gets a chance to take the point, by huddling with his or her family and deciding on an answer. If neither student is correct, we do a bonus round, and both groups huddle and offer one more answer. If no one gets the correct answer after all that, I tell them the answer, we talk about it briefly, and we begin again with the next two members of the families.

Effectiveness. This is a great attention getter, because students work overtime to assist each other in understanding and obtaining the answers. It is also a great tool for me to see what concepts I may need to go over again with the class or with individual students. By the time this activity is complete, students have usually mastered the material, and they breeze through the test.

DEBRIEF OF LESSON 3

In the first two lessons, students were *directly* coaching and teaching each other as they learned about a new concept. The distinction in this lesson is that the focus of attention has shifted, and students are *indirectly* helping each other to review and process information. When working indirectly to help each other, students are often unaware of the amount of effort they are expending. Since their conscious focus is on something else, they are distracted from possibly thinking, "This is too much work!" or "I don't want to review again, that's so boring!" The social dynamic of working together allows them to engage fully in the lesson.

In general, TV game shows can be a useful configuration to allow students to learn indirectly, especially for review sessions. Lesson 7 in the chapter on novelty demonstrates another use of a TV game show, as does this next demonstration, which incorporates a clever twist on the whole game show idea.

LESSON 4

Using artifacts to trigger social interactions between students

Topic	"Survivor" Recall
Students	Fourth Grade: ages 9–10
Primary Green Light strategy	Socialization
Related strategies	Memory, novelty, emotion, and movement
Submitted by	Kim Cooke, PE and Health Teacher
	Union County Schools
	Monroe, North Carolina

Red Light. Traditionally, students receive a review sheet and work independently to study for a test the next day.

Green Light. Suppose we are reviewing the substance abuse unit. I place all the artifacts or posters that have been used in the unit throughout the classroom to serve as memory triggers. When the music starts—we use the theme song to *Survivor*—students work in pairs or trios to visit each "tribal stop" and discuss why the artifact or poster is displayed. For this particular lesson, here are a few artifacts and posters I use:

1. Pictures of rat poison, nail polish, butane, and insecticides (students recall that these are all ingredients found in cigarettes)

2. A sign that says "0.08" (students recall that the legal limit to drive is 0.08 or lower in North Carolina)

3. Tobacco ads (students recall the lesson on how tobacco companies advertise products by making them appeal cool, refreshing, smooth, and so forth)

4. Pictures of a healthy lung and a non-healthy lung (students discuss long-term effects from smoking)

5. A poster or sign that states, "Name five short-term effects from smoking"

6. A poster that says "23 minutes" (students recall that every 23 minutes someone is killed by a drunk driver)

7. A poster or sign that states, "Name five short-term effects from smokeless tobacco"

8. A poster of Gruen Von Behrens (students recall the video they watched of a teenager named Gruen who got cancer from smokeless tobacco)

Effectiveness. Student engagement is high! Students feed off of each other as they recall the memories of the unit associated with each item. I quite often hear students say to each other, "Oh yeah, I remember that" or "This was when we were talking about..." I can assess student learning by listening to their dialogue and ask them questions as I move throughout the room.

DEBRIEF OF LESSON 4

The distinctive characteristic of this lesson is the use of physical objects—artifacts or posters—to stimulate the small group conversations. In the "Connections" chapter, Lesson 2 talks about using artifacts to teach a lesson or introduce a concept. Here, the focus is specifically on having artifacts used in previous lessons trigger student discussions. With an artifact or poster as a starting point to trigger recall, conversations usually take off immediately.

In this lesson, artifacts are being used as part of the review process; however, they could also be used to *introduce* a lesson. Perhaps the teacher sets out the artifacts and posters and invites students to wander around with their friends and talk about each item: what it might mean, why it might be a part of the lesson. This technique would trigger students' prior knowledge, providing an excellent platform from which to dive into the depths of the actual lesson.

When used this way, the artifacts *reflect* the concepts. The whole notion of reflection can be taken a step further, as in this next lesson, where the concept is taught in a social setting that *mirrors* where the learning will later be used.

LESSON 5

Matching the social setting of the learning to the social setting of the application

Topic	Making Change
Students	Second Grade: ages 7–8
Primary Green Light strategy	Socialization
Related strategies	Visuals, drama, and novelty
Submitted by	Peggy Frum, Second-Grade Teacher
	Gulliver Academy
	Miami, Florida

Red Light. Traditionally, students use a workbook or textbook with pictures of coins and a story problem. They calculate the amount of change needed by counting on their fingers, using the pictures, and writing the number values under each coin.

Green Light. I have students work with partners, sitting somewhere in the room beside each other. One student is the "cashier" and the other student is the "customer." The cashier has a bag of play money and a toy, and the customer has another bag of money. The teacher then reads a story about shopping such as, "Johnny had two quarters. He wanted to buy a toy duck that cost $0.34. He gave the cashier his two quarters. What change did he receive?"

The cashier gives the toy duck to the customer, and the customer hands the two quarters to the clerk and waits for change. The cashier makes the change and counts it out to the customer while placing each coin in the customer's hand. The customer then declares how much change he received. The teacher reviews the addition/ subtraction work on the board. Students reverse roles for the next problem.

Effectiveness. This has been a great way to teach counting when making change. Previously, students had a difficult time realizing the value of the change when it was only on paper. Having actual coins in their hands helps them see the value of the change by physically counting out the money. The fact that this is an *actual social transaction* they have seen their parents do before—and will see again—adds a significant layer of understanding and importance to the lesson.

DEBRIEF OF LESSON 5

The teacher in this lesson has created an exact match to a real-life social circumstance that students are familiar with. If this content is taught by the traditional pencil-and-paper method, students may fail to transfer what they've learned from concept to reality, and if they cannot apply the information within the appropriate context, little real learning has occurred. However, when information is taught using a simulation of the skill's social context, they are more likely to be able to transfer their abstract understanding of the concept into useful reality.

Creating a *matching social situation* has a great deal of potential for increasing student learning. For example:

- Art: Is it possible that someday someone will ask students their opinion of a piece of art? If so, create that scenario and let them practice how they could respond. What do they like, and why? Encourage them to use words they've been learning in class.
- History: Do they ever have guests from out of town who might ask them questions about where they live? If so, see how they will respond if someone asks, "What's the oldest building in town?" or "When was this city established?" or maybe even "Are there any really cool graveyards?" Asking each other these questions in the classroom would be far more dynamic that simply writing down the answers on a sheet of paper.
- Earth science: Using the same idea, get them to respond to questions such as, "How much rain do you get here?" or "What's that tree called?" or "Why aren't there any bears in the woods here?"

Learning a concept within the bounds of its appropriate social setting will increase the students' ability to recall it later when the *matching social situation* arises.

This idea is explicitly demonstrated in the next lesson, where the social setting of the classroom itself becomes the matching social setting of the learning process.

LESSON 6

Students becoming the teachers

Topic	Science and Social Studies
Students	Fourth Grade: ages 9–10
Primary Green Light strategy	Socialization

Related strategies	Connections, visuals, movement, and novelty
Submitted by	Jenn Currie, Fourth-Grade Teacher
	Commodore Perry School
	Hadley, Pennsylvania

Red Light. Traditionally, students sit in rows of desks and listen to a lecture on science or social studies for the entire 40-minute period.

Green Light. Students are paired up and encouraged to find a place in the room to work together, on the floor, at a small table, or in the corners of the room. Each partnership is given a scavenger hunt for a particular lesson in the book. One person is the designated "reader"—the one who reads the content aloud and the other person is the "scribe"—the one who writes down what they find. Halfway through the scavenger hunt, they exchange roles. After a set amount of time, all class members reconvene, and each pair briefly teaches the rest of the class about what they discovered during their hunt.

Effectiveness. This has been a great way to give ownership to the students. Sometimes—believe it or not—they get tired of hearing me talk! This way, they can learn equally as well, while having the opportunity to chatter away happily with each other. Allowing them to work together by reading and searching for the answers also allows them to gain a deeper understanding of the subject matter because they need to manipulate the material to answer some of the more intricate questions.

DEBRIEF OF LESSON 6

Allowing groups of students to become the "teachers" can have numerous beneficial side effects. Some of these are as follows:

- It's novel.
- It's a more memorable lesson.
- It allows the students to make their own connections to the material.
- They get to talk to each other as they look through the materials.
- Engagement levels—and thus processing levels—are significantly higher than they would be from simply listening to the teacher talk.
- From their presentations, the teacher can assess what they know and add in whatever they may have overlooked.

Many students take great pleasure in playing the role of the teacher. One high school math teacher reported that throughout the year, he occasionally offered an automatic A on a chapter to any student who worked together with one or two other students to teach that chapter to the rest of the class. Some groups accepted this offer, delighted at being given the opportunity to avoid taking the test for that chapter. However, without realizing it, these students often expended huge amounts of extra time and energy preparing lesson plans, delivering the content, and devising and grading the test for the other students—much more than they would have if they were playing their normal student role. As a result of interacting with their peers, through preparing, presenting, and elaborating on the information, they had a very clear understanding of the content.

Giving students a chance to become the teacher in this particular manner is not an entirely "hands-off" endeavor for the real teacher. Time will need to be spent supporting the group of student teachers throughout the process, overseeing their level of preparedness and verifying their level of accuracy in understanding the content. At times, however, the cost of the time spent may indeed equal the reward.

Although some of the above examples are quite involved, social learning doesn't have to be complicated. Many lessons can be simple and elegant, in both design and execution, while still tapping into the benefits generated by bringing more social interaction into the classroom. In this final example, by adding just one simple strategy, a normally quiet activity transforms into a lively, student-driven, interaction-oriented lesson.

LESSON 7

Students working together to help each other learn and understand

Topic	Spelling: "Scrambled Eggs"
Students	First and Second Grades: ages 6–8
Primary Green Light strategy	Socialization
Related strategies	Movement, visuals, and novelty
Submitted by	Shari Rindels, First-Grade Teacher
	Catalina Ventura School
	Phoenix, Arizona

Red Light. Traditionally, when students learn how to scramble and unscramble words to spell them correctly, a teacher demonstrates it by showing flash cards. An alternative is to use the whiteboard or chalkboard to first write the word, next write the letters scrambled up, and finally show the students how to unscramble them to make the correct word. Students come up to the board individually or work quietly at their seat with paper and pencil to practice.

Green Light. After learning how to unscramble words together, instead of doing seat work we play "Scrambled Eggs." I hold up a big Easter basket filled with decorated plastic eggs, and we talk about the fun of going on an Easter egg hunt. Then I tell the students that—believe it or not—we are going to use these Easter eggs to learn how to spell our words better.

Pairs of students each get an egg, crack it open, scramble up the letters inside, and then work together to unscramble those letters to make one of their spelling words. When a pair is done, both students stand up, and I come around and check to see it they are right. If the word is right, they get a "thumbs up," put the egg back together, and trade eggs with somebody else until the egg timer goes off and all eggs are returned to the basket.

Effectiveness. Students love Scrambled Eggs day—energy levels rise at the beginning of our spelling lesson each Wednesday when the Easter basket comes out. Students love working together to unscramble the letters and find the secret word!

DEBRIEF OF LESSON 7

One of the keys to being an effective Green Light teacher is to take any effective teaching strategy and discover *alternative application options*. Consider the essentials of the Scrambled Eggs idea on a broader scale, across various age levels and subjects. What else could be written on slips of paper and hidden in plastic eggs?

In a foreign language class, could there be scrambled vocabulary words? In science, English, or social studies classes, could there be a word and three possible definitions? In a history class, could there be an important historical event and four dates? In a math class, could there be math problems with five possible answers? In *any* age-level class, students could crack open an egg and be asked to

- Create a chronological timeline of facts for any era of social studies
- Sequence the stages of the life cycle of a plant or animal
- Sort the parts of a flower, cell, or *anything* into the proper diagram
- Arrange fractions in order from least to greatest
- Match math problems with the correct answer
- Match words with their definitions

The potential variations of this seemingly simple teaching strategy are truly endless, yet each would require students to be engaged socially as they tackle the assignment.

Student Conversations: The Fundamental Question

In the ocean of possibilities surrounding social learning, many teachers have an undercurrent of uncertainty, a ripple of disquiet, perhaps even

WE CONSTRUCT INFORMATION SOCIALLY

a tidal wave of anxiety concerning student-to-student social interactions. Their big question is,

Will they go off task?

Let us tackle this question head-on. The answer is,

Absolutely yes, most definitely!

The truth is that most students will at least occasionally veer off course during social interaction, caught in a riptide of conversations that are relevant to them, but not at all relevant to the content. The key here is to recognize that, if this happens, students probably *weren't thinking about the lesson anyway*. In this case, allowing them to talk to each other gives them a chance to express their thoughts, opinions, and feelings, and release that pent-up energy. Once the conversation has run its course, they will return their focus to the classroom and the topic at hand and hopefully pay attention to the lesson.

Does this mean it's always OK for them to drift off into purely social conversations? Certainly not! However, it may not be such a terrible thing in the context of the overall learning process. Green Light teachers recognize that these perfectly natural moments happen in all classrooms, with all ages of students, whenever social interaction is permitted. The key is to read the group's level of distraction and act accordingly (Mercer & Sams, 2006). If they need to talk, let them do what they need to do!

Perhaps the most important point is that if we *don't* allow these conversations to occur, students may very well end up doing them anyway, by side talking, whispering, or passing notes. When their focus goes south like this, they definitely aren't focusing on the lesson!

Green Light teachers would rather students get this stuff out of their systems during moments of classroom socialization than have them running as a perpetual, disruptive undercurrent. They recognize that students are human—that attention levels rise and fall, and that no one can fully pay attention for every second of a whole hour. By respecting the human need for social interaction and deliberately including it in our teaching strategies, we can turn students' potentially disruptive tendency to chat into a powerful learning tool.

KEY POINTS

- Students need frequent breaks to talk to each other and "download." This allows them to clear their mind for subsequent intake of new ideas.
- Social interactions where students help each other can be wonderful. Be cautious about the setup, however, never implying students are either "smart" or "dumb."
- When students work together to discover new information, there's a powerful feeling of success, leading to a deeper level of connection with the material.
- To be most effective, students should work together in a *variety of formats*.
- Having pairs *mismatch* the information can be a novel way to socialize.
- Social interactions can be focused *directly* on the content, or *indirectly*, where groups participate in game show style review sessions.
- Artifacts can stimulate group conversations and interactions.
- A *matching social situation* spices up a lesson and increases the chance of students' being able to apply the information in real life.
- When students become "teachers," they learn too.
- Student conversations always drift off topic. It's natural and normal. Allow them to complete their discussion, and then guide them back on topic.

QUESTIONS TO ASK YOURSELF

- Are you willing to let your students interact with each other more frequently?
- How can you balance situations where students directly help each other with ones where they indirectly assist each other in learning new concepts and ideas?
- How does the concept of a *matching social situation* fit with your subject area?
- Which specific topics are naturally more open for having students become the teachers?
- How do you plan to handle the moment when students go off task during a group discussion? It *will* happen, so be prepared!

9 Drama

All the world's a stage—especially the classroom.

How will you use them in your lessons?

ADAPT . . . ADJUST . . . APPLY

Does this happen in your classroom? Lessons are occasionally presented with dramatic flair. Aided by the teacher, students become scriptwriters, set designers, directors, and actors. Content springs to life through dramatic presentations. Understanding deepens as performers and audience alike "live" the material. Unforgettable performances create lasting lessons.

DRAMA: AN OVERVIEW

The vast universe of the dramatic experience is exciting to both young and old. At least once in their lives, most people have been enthralled by a play or movie that captivated their attention and relentlessly drew them in. For a short time, they surrendered to the thrill of suspended belief, caught up in the magic of the experience. And they never forgot that moment. Some of us have been fortunate enough to feel the thrill of creating that magic for an audience. But, whether as an observer or as a participant, each of us inherently understands the power and majesty drama has to entertain us, to move us, and to teach us things we will never forget.

Fortunately for teachers, if we peek backstage, the magic of a dramatic presentation depends on some clear and practical elements. We can isolate these elements, include them in our lesson plans, and use the dynamic experience of drama to make lessons both highly enjoyable and memorable for our students (Reid, 2000).

For example, any dramatic presentation needs a story and a script. It also needs writers, directors, and of course, actors and actresses. Other elements are optional. Props help. Costumes help. A set helps. Yet a teacher with even with the barest resources can easily use drama to create magic for students—bringing dry material to vibrant life.

While many teachers understand the value of including at least some elements of drama in the classroom, some find it hard to see how to do that without creating a full-blown play, with sets, lights, costumes, and late-afternoon rehearsals. No one has time to do that more than once a year—it is simply too time-consuming, and time is a scarce enough resource in most classrooms.

The point is, when we incorporate drama into instruction, the actual moments of learning can occur in rehearsal, behind the scenes, or onstage—and the performance itself can be as simple as a two-minute sketch with minimal props. We can incorporate learning in every part of dramatic development. In planning, students must understand the material before they can decide how to tell a story. Writing and rehearsing are excellent learning vehicles as students have to carefully review and think about the content. In performances, the actors, the crew, and the audience all learn—the actors and crew because their heightened emotional state strongly embeds the memories, and the audience because the message is encoded in visuals and emotion. Even after the performance, learning continues, as the experience triggers further discussions among the cast, crew, and audience.

Guided properly, drama can trigger a wealth of healthy emotions and positive learning for everyone involved in any aspect of the production, large or small. We have a wide range of options for building the various elements of drama into a lesson, as the following lessons so brilliantly show. They demonstrate applications across the range of dramatic presentation that can be adapted to any group of students and any subject.

So let's raise the curtain on a few of these wonderful lessons and discover some of the many possibilities for connecting the natural joy of dramatic engagement with the learning process.

LESSON 1

Learning through creating, practicing, performing, and debriefing skits

Topic	Pre– through Post–American Revolutionary Period
Students	Eighth Grade: ages 13–14
Primary Green Light strategy	Drama
Related strategies	Movement, tone, and novelty
Submitted by	Greg Rayer, Eighth-Grade Teacher
	Mary Queen of the Holy Rosary School
	Lexington, Kentucky

Red Light. Traditionally, students read a chapter, and the teacher delivers a lecture—or perhaps shows a DVD. Questions are answered, and students take a test.

Green Light. I divide our class into groups of five or six students. Each group is required to perform a vignette: a short skit that depicts one of the events from the American Revolutionary period. Examples include the Boston Massacre; the Boston Tea Party; the Midnight Ride of Revere, Dawes, and Prescott; Ethan Allen and Benedict Arnold capturing Fort Ticonderoga; the Battle of Saratoga and French support of the Americans; the Declaration of Independence; Winter at Valley Forge; and the British Surrender at Yorktown.

These mini-dramas have to be short, no more than five minutes. Students have to write out scripts, and everyone has to be in all vignettes. Students can use props, costumes, and music for special effects. Classes are required to research their four topics and be as historically correct as possible. I give the students three class periods to prepare, with presentations on the fourth day. At the conclusion of each group's presentations, we discuss the material presented for historical accuracy and significance.

Effectiveness. *Test scores for the classes that studied using this format were dramatically higher* than the scores in three other classes taught right next door using traditional Red Light strategies!

DEBRIEF OF LESSON 1

One of the simplest—and often most effective—ways to bring drama into the classroom is to invite students to perform skits based on the content (Cruz & Murthy, 2006). Using this approach, the teacher's role is to isolate the events students need to focus on and provide support materials for their productions, such as a box of props or perhaps a few costumes. The teacher then steps back and lets the natural learning process take over. The point is that to create their skits, students must engage with and understand the material—so they can't help but learn it. Their eagerness to perform, and the subtle pressure from their peers in their group, means they will almost always rise to the occasion.

We have many options to engage students in the skit process. Sometimes only a few students from the group need actually perform, while everyone else helps in preparation and planning. Alternatively, students could merely write scripts and *read* skits, not actually act them out—relieving the pressure to memorize lines. Alternatively, if there's no time for script writing, students can simply act out a scene without words. This is more complex than normal charades: the object here is for the other students not to simply guess correctly, but to verify the accuracy of the mimed demonstration. Again, the students creating the skit will process the material at a more complex level than they would if the information was delivered in a lecture.

Mike Boshka, a Green Light English teacher at Bigfork High School, Bigfork, Montana, has created his own, highly popular variation on performing skits. Each student is given a Pez dispenser from a collection he keeps in the classroom and then groups are assigned a section of *Macbeth* to act out—using the Pez dispensers as the characters in the scene. Students have a blast making their Pez characters speak, walk, talk, and occasionally even perform fight scenes. Their performances lead to discussions concerning many of the critical aspects of the tragedy itself, such as the motivations of the characters or the many questions of right and wrong. The resulting high levels of engagement lead to lively conversations and, again, deeper processing of the material than a lecture format might allow.

With *Macbeth*, the lines are already written so the characters merely act them out, which allows students to move to the dramatic interpretive process more quickly. The following lesson puts this same idea to use, but with a twist.

LESSON 2

Acting out song lyrics to convey key content

Topic	German History
Students	High school: ages 14–18
Primary Green Light strategy	Drama
Related strategies	Movement, emotion, socialization, and novelty
Submitted by	Katie Sloan, Biology and German Teacher
	Bishop Kelley High School
	Tulsa, Oklahoma

Red Light. The German song *"Sind so kleine Hände,"* written by Bettina Wegner, is a striking example of how lyrics were used in the former German Democratic Republic to convey more than one meaning. On the surface, the song is a great lullaby and has many concrete thoughts regarding children and their little eyes and mouths. The abstract undertones, which increase in complexity as the song moves forward, tell a tale of oppression and of a yearning—if not a pleading—for society to change. Previously, I would let the students read the text aloud and we would translate it as a class. Then I would try to explain everything I've just explained here. It didn't work very well.

Green Light. I gave them the song text and asked them to divide into groups of two or three. I then assigned each group a certain number of stanzas to act out. After the groups had put their parts together, they demonstrated them for the class and taught the other groups the movements they used. After we all learned the movements, I asked questions about what other possible meanings or stories there might be, given the author's choice of words. I didn't have to ask too many questions, because once they began acting out the song, the hidden meanings started to show themselves.

Effectiveness. This was such a dynamic experience for both the students and me as the teacher! The students remembered the artist's choice of words and phrasing, even though I didn't ask them to memorize the song. This was also a great way to learn new vocabulary, and I doubt they'll soon forget it. We then went on to talk about what life was like in the German Democratic Republic. It was a *great* day for everyone.

DEBRIEF OF LESSON 2

In this lesson, as in the first one, students were the actors. Here, however, instead of performing a written play, they acted out the words to a song. Some songs may have deep levels of learning, as in the example in this lesson, while others may be simply for enjoyment to complement a topic and make it more memorable. For example, students studying earthquakes might act out "Shake, Rattle, and Roll" by Bill Haley and the Comets, or "I Feel the Earth Move Under My Feet" by Carole King. Many more ideas for both of these types of songs can be found in *The Green Book of Songs by Subject* (Green, 2002).

This teacher also makes an extremely important note when she states, "I didn't have to ask too many questions, because once they began acting out the song, the hidden meanings started to show themselves." What she has discovered is that whether the words are from a song, a play, a book, or even a regular textbook, when students act out the words, they frequently understand the writer's intention much more clearly (Pierce & Terry, 2000). The next lesson takes this idea one step further, as students actually *become* the content they are learning!

LESSON 3

Learning through involvement by becoming the content

Topic	Subtraction
Students	First Grade: ages 6–7
Primary Green Light strategy	Drama
Related strategies	Movement, novelty, connections, and memory
Submitted by	Kristine Sobbe, First- and Second-Grade Teacher
	Goose Bay Elementary School
	Wasilla, Alaska

Red Light. Traditionally, teachers hand out a worksheet and tell students what subtraction is and how to do it. The Red Light teacher would show a bunch of examples, hoping that the students would understand the process of subtraction and the procedure of how to do the math problems.

Green Light. When we learn about subtraction, we role-play. It is easier for students to understand something that they are doing actively, so we create the problem out of people. We have seven people standing up at one end of the front of the classroom, and four people at the other. I then tell them that the group of four needs to go and take away one person each from the group of seven. When that occurs, we have our "product." This is the first exposure that most of these students have had to subtraction, and it is a very memorable one.

We practice this type of subtraction for a few days, moving from teacher-taught subtraction problems to student-taught subtraction problems. The students act as the teacher, telling the "subtraction problem" where to move. Only when they have done a week of moving subtraction do we introduce the written form of subtraction.

Effectiveness. This physical moving subtraction helps students understand what they are doing when they subtract before they even look at what a subtraction problem on paper looks like. It creates a mental image that helps students to understand math instead of simply memorizing it. From this solid foundation of their understanding of this concept, we can move easily into more advanced topics.

DEBRIEF OF LESSON 3

This lesson demonstrates a novel twist on the student-centered theme. Instead of acting out the content, they become the content. Math has multiple opportunities for students to become numbers, operations, answers, and formulas. Math can be a conceptual, abstract topic, and students who are kinesthetically oriented—meaning they prefer to learn through physical engagement—may struggle to understand the material. However, if taught using dramatic engagement, these students may well learn the concepts much more rapidly because the teaching process matches their orientation to the world.

Math is not the only topic where this will work. Consider an English class. Perhaps students could become nouns, pronouns, prepositions, verbs, adjectives, and other key types of words. Perhaps they could then form a line, based on what kind of word they are, to create a grammatically correct sentence. In music class, perhaps students could become musical notes and act out a musical sequence. In a history class, perhaps students could become dates, locations, or form timelines. All the teacher has to do is find a way for the students to physically become the content.

In these first three lessons, elements of drama were used to help teach concepts and ideas. But is it possible to do drama-based assessments?

LESSON 4

Role-playing used as a form of assessment

Topic	Learning the Muscle Groups
Students	High school: ages 14–18

Primary Green Light strategy	Drama
Related strategies	Memory, novelty, and socialization
Submitted by	Karen Renaud, High School PE Teacher
	Ashland High School
	Ashland, Massachusetts

Red Light. Students learn the major muscle groups, how to safely use the fitness equipment, and how to perform exercises by observing the teacher as she demonstrates, taking notes and reading descriptions.

Green Light. I demonstrate an exercise and then ask a student to repeat the demonstration while I explain. I tell the students which muscle groups are being used and physically touch those muscles. Students are then instructed to touch that muscle group on themselves, and then *respectfully* on a few friends. They say things like, "Hey, nice latissimus dorsi!" We then add to that by putting the name of the exercise with the muscle group. They become "temporary actors" and may approach at least three people and say, "Did you know that the Lat Pull Down will really develop your latissimus dorsi?" Students then practice the exercise with a partner and explain how to do it to one another.

For assessment, I have them play the role of "personal trainer" rather than give a written test. They are asked to properly train their "client" to perform an exercise. They must tell the client the name of the exercise, tell which muscles it works, demonstrate how to perform it correctly, monitor their client as they perform the exercise and make any necessary corrections, and tell their client how many repetitions and how much weight will be used. Basically, while acting as the personal trainer, they are explaining everything that I want them to know.

Effectiveness. I have found this approach to be extremely effective. With the old Red Light approach, I could get through a three-week unit and still have half of my students not understanding what they were doing and why they were doing it. With the Green Light approach, I find that students learn the muscle groups much more quickly because we do it in a fun, relaxed, and physical manner. They also gain a better understanding of the "how-tos" and "whys" of the exercises. I explain and model, and then they model, practice, and get it into their bodies. They talk about it and role-play it as the personal trainer—and learn the material!

DEBRIEF OF LESSON 4

This lesson demonstrates a further twist on the basic idea of students acting out the content. Here the teacher is actually assessing student learning through role-playing. How many different ways could we use this strategy? While any teacher would most likely want to include occasional written assessments as a part of his or her instruction, this alternative approach might very well be more effective for some of the students, allowing those who don't always do well on the typical written test a chance to show what they know in a very valid format. For a variation on this theme of creative assessment, see Lesson 1 in the next chapter, on visuals, where students assess their *own* work.

In the next lesson, we return to students learning through drama, only this time they are doing it in a very different form.

LESSON 5

Creating a multimedia production as a means of learning content

Topic	Pollution
Students	Second and Third Grades: ages 7–9
Primary Green Light strategy	Drama
Related strategies	Visuals, tone, and novelty
Submitted by	Sheryl Fainges, Year 2 Teacher
	Manly West State School
	Manly West, Queensland, Australia

Red Light. Traditionally, teaching "Society and the Environment" employs a textbook approach with some library and Internet research. A Red Light teacher would also use the blackboard or whiteboard, charts, and other paper handouts to instruct the students about the impact of pollution on the environment.

Green Light. My Year 1 students created a pollution video. They designed two pollution characters by stapling old chip bags, straws, juice boxes, and papers onto some sacks. A simple hole was cut into the top of the sack, which allowed the garment to sit over the head and on the shoulders. Simple masks were made to hide the faces of the students playing the roles of Mr. and Mrs. Pollution.

The students wrote a simple script (based on the silent movies of the Keystone Cops) and chose several sites for the video: the classroom, the environmental area, the eating area, and the parade ground. Students rotated through the role of Mr. and Mrs. Pollution and the Good Guys. I videotaped the students' play using a digital video camera. A technical assistant helped with downloading and editing the video while the Year 1 students instructed him on what they wanted to include.

Effectiveness. The activity covered a range of learning strategies and provided hands-on experience in both designing and producing a play. Disengaged students actively participated throughout the project. Several subject areas were covered, and students freely engaged in their own research at home and at school. It provided greater meaning for young students as they explored the impact of pollution within their school environment. Having viewed the video, we went on to talk about healthy eating at school and ways to keep our school clean.

DEBRIEF OF LESSON 5

In this situation, the format of the production and the presentation has changed, from a live play to a video. Typically, when video is the medium, students want to practice many times before they are taped, creating multiple opportunities for learning. In addition, every time video is viewed, the lesson is repeated. As students proudly share their video with their friends, parents, and extended family, and view it again and again throughout the year, their learning and recall get stronger and stronger.

A live play often uses only one physical location, although the scenery may be changed occasionally. However, as the teacher mentions, using video as the production medium provides opportunities for a variety of stages—different areas for learning (Moreno & Mayer, 2000). This means students will experience the content on a much broader scale, and perhaps make wider connections to the information and how it applies to the real world. For another example of how to utilize this idea, see Lesson 3 in the "Connections" chapter.

Video expands the horizons of dramatic possibilities. Indeed, TV itself can frequently provide the creative spark to trigger new and novel ways to include variations of drama in teaching, as shown in the next lesson.

LESSON 6

Creating and performing a talk show based on content

Topic	Literature Representation of a Book
Students	Fifth Grade: ages 10–11
Primary Green Light strategy	Drama
Related strategies	Novelty, tone, and emotion
Submitted by	Jenn Currie, Fourth-Grade Teacher
	Commodore Perry School
	Hadley, Pennsylvania

Red Light. Traditionally, at the end of a novel, students would be given the choice of creating a scripted book report or a diorama. They would turn it in to the teacher to be graded. End of story.

Green Light. After literature groups complete a novel, I give them several options on how to share the plot of their book with the rest of the class. Recently, a popular choice has been to create and put on a talk show. Normally, I allow a maximum of five students per group. One student becomes the host, and the remaining students become the characters in the book.

They work together on questions the host should ask that are relevant to the plot of the story. They also create reactions and answers to those questions just as the characters would have answered them. When possible, these students also dress the part of each character. The students also frequently use music as an accompaniment as each character is invited onto the "stage."

Effectiveness. This has been a great way to see how much meaning each student got from the book, with students' comprehension being quite evident in the way they constructed questions and answers for the interviews. Watching how they portrayed each character also provided evidence that they were connecting with the characters. They did this all on their own … with no help from me at all! *It was truly amazing!* A jaw-dropping experience.

DEBRIEF OF LESSON 6

Here's yet another creative way to use drama: putting on a talk show! Instead of asking the students for a written review, this teacher has opened the door for verbal and dramatic commentary. In doing so, the students have engaged with the material at a much deeper level, increasing their understanding and insight. This verbal mode also allows students to significantly enhance their vocabulary (Sutton, 1998).

Once again, there are many possible variations of this basic theme. For example, in some situations, maybe the talk show goes as planned for a few minutes, and then the audience—other students—could come up with additional questions to ask the characters. Or maybe the teacher generates a series of basic questions she might ask the characters, and students form groups and plan how they would answer each question if they were that character—and then the show goes on. Or, would the reverse be possible? Could the *teacher* become a character, with the students getting to ask questions and then having to decide whether the character was being truthful? The only way they'd know the right answers is if they understood the book!

This simple talk show approach could be used many times in a single year with students never tiring of it since the format can vary so easily. One of these variations, though, puts the teacher momentarily in the spotlight, and this next lesson extends that idea further.

LESSON 7

The teacher becoming the star performer to convey content

Topic	Place Value of Large Numbers
Students	Third–Sixth Grades: ages 8–12
Primary Green Light strategy	Drama

Related strategies   Tone, novelty, emotion, and socialization
Submitted by   Tiffany Reindl, Fifth- and Sixth-Grade Teacher
                                          Jefferson School for the Arts
                                          Stevens Point, Wisconsin

Red Light. Most Red Light strategies would present this information in the form of a chart, which would allow the students to perform the skill—maybe—as long as they had the chart to refer to.

Green Light. So much of our math unit was based on knowing place value, I knew I had to develop a memorable way for my students to recall the information. I wanted to do something to set this information apart from the rest. Most of my students had prior knowledge of number values up to ten thousands, but were new to larger numbers.

As my students filed in for math class under the watchful eye of an educational assistant, they discovered an independent review assignment written on the board. A few students inquired about my absence but soon got to work. About five minutes later, I stumbled into class, breathing hard, swaddled in elastic bandages, and acting like I was in a death scene of a really bad movie. Someone in my caring class managed to ask what was up between giggles and jokes. I delivered my story with the accompanying hand motions.

> I was going to my car to get a bag when a truck came. One (hold up one finger) truck ran over my toes a thousand times! Wait, it gets worse! Then it turned around and ran over my middle (point to stomach) a million times and stopped! I had to use my bulging biceps (flex arm muscle) to push the billion-ton truck off of me. Calling help a trillion times was at the tip of my tongue (stick out tongue and point to it) but I didn't want to overreact (hand to forehead in classic swoon pose).

Then, with as much sincerity as I can muster, I say, "What? It really happened! Let me tell you again." I repeat the story, stressing the key words.

I then challenge the students to work with a partner to figure out why I told this story. I'm not afraid of silly answers, because it creates a fun tone in the room. After they've talked for a few minutes, I start to write *one, thousand, million, billion,* and *trillion* on the board, which brings the students back to topic. Explaining to them that when writing or reading large numbers they have a cheat sheet on their body, I have everyone stand up to use it. With a proper finger extended, we say "one." They tap their toes on the ground and say, "thousands," pat their middles and say "millions," flex an arm and say "billions," and put their hands to their mouths like they were yelling and say "trillions." We repeat this routine a few times until it takes on the feel of a chant. As I proceed with the lesson, anytime a student gets stuck on reading a number, I just do the body actions as a form of reinforcement. The following day, I review the story again by saying "Remember that day I got hit by a truck?"

Effectiveness. This lesson is effective for several reasons—the dramatic presentation in the beginning, the silliness used to teach it, and the application of a solid memory technique—storytelling. Math is usually so straitlaced that it is unusual to be this absurd when teaching it. The body actions make for a stronger memory recall. The initial letters of the body parts correspond to the first letter of the place value, acting like an acronym. This activity was so memorable that the following year, students were telling their new teacher about it as they reviewed the topic of place values.

DEBRIEF OF LESSON 7

In this example, a new aspect of drama has been introduced: the teacher has become the primary performer. In this particular example, of course, the teacher is going to extremes, which some teachers may not feel comfortable with. However, whether or not we choose to go to these lengths in our performance, we can have the same effect on the students by making even minor variations from our usual selves—perhaps by doing an accent, talking in a funny voice, wearing just one significant piece of a costume, such as a hat, or using a prop. Even these simple dramatic elements can bring a potentially mundane lesson to dramatic life. Indeed, it has been said that

Teaching is one quarter preparation and three quarters presentation.

It is certainly the intention of this chapter to validate that claim. Despite the best preparation by the teacher, if the presentation is not interesting, the students will rarely get much value from the lesson. Yet with only a little preparation, what engages the students, what captivates and motivates them, is the energy and dynamics of the performance. Teachers should feel free to take full dramatic license and step boldly into any dramatic role they are willing to explore. The courage to do this comes from the certain knowledge that, by doing so, they are helping their students learn at a much deeper level.

Occasionally a Green Light teacher might want to go all the way, combining all the elements of drama discussed so far to create a play that can be enjoyed by the students as they learn the content. . . .

LESSON 8

Creating an entire play around content in which everyone can be engaged

Topic   The Rock Cycle
Students   Fifth Grade: ages 10–11

Primary Green Light strategy	Drama
Related strategies	Tone, memory, movement, and visuals
Submitted by	Emma Jeter, Fifth-Grade Teacher
	Christopher Farms Elementary School
	Virginia Beach, Virginia

Red Light. Traditionally, we would use the science textbook to learn about what happens to rocks. We would look at some examples of different types of rocks and discuss how one rock could change into another. Students would look in the textbook and then create a poster with a diagram of the rock cycle. They would then be asked to memorize the rock cycle in time for the test.

Green Light. In general, students love to be onstage. I couldn't find a play about the rock cycle, so *I wrote one*! Everyone auditioned for parts, memorized their lines, and rehearsed onstage. I also wrote a song that we sing to the tune of "Hangin' Tough" by New Kids on the Block. Our song is called "The Rock Cycle Rock." We practiced the play and sang the song as part of the play.* Eventually we did a performance for the entire school and even invited parents to attend!

Once they have performed the play and song, I then give them a big piece of paper and ask them to design their own diagram of the rock cycle. They already have all the information needed for the test memorized.

Effectiveness. Students always want to do a great job in front of each other, and especially in front of the school onstage. Every student has a part in the play and plenty of stage time. They are always excited about the song. The rock cycle posters they produce are of a much higher standard than in my previous years of teaching this material, and they are ready for the test after the performance without having to review! It's awesome!

DEBRIEF OF LESSON 8

This example has been included as the final lesson with the full understanding that most teachers simply don't have the time, energy, or resources to go this far, creating an entire play and song. However, if this *is* occasionally possible, it can be an incredible learning opportunity for everyone involved. Perhaps just once or twice a year, for very special content areas, all Green Light teachers should consider this as a possibility. Remember, after it's created once, it can be performed for many more years! And each year it will naturally grow and develop, so while the first year might just be a modest, five- to seven-minute creation, over time it will evolve into a full-blown play!

---

*For the text of the full play and the song lyrics, see the Appendix.

Our Inner Actor/Actress . . . and the Gift

When presented with the chance to be involved in a dramatic production, some students will leap forward eagerly, while others, particularly older students, may be more resistant to, and perhaps even frightened of, the opportunity. The question arises regarding whether we should push them, and if so, how far?

The belief that we all have an inner actor or actress comes from the fact that as kids almost all of us role-play to a considerable extent. It's natural for young kids to have vast imaginations and the unfettered willingness to take on any role. Most imaginary games involve young children becoming police officers, cowboys, mothers, and doctors. For a while, these kids love nothing better than to pretend to be animals. Sometimes they go even further and are willing to become *inanimate* objects: rocks, paper clips, or walls. In the beginning, there's no doubt that, at some level, all of us have a seed of drama deep inside ourselves.

Yet as we grow older, and our personalities develop, the *form* of this expression often adjusts and matures. Some people, of course, will be willing hams their entire lives, eager to leap onstage at a moment's notice! Yet others may choose to walk a different path, finding their self-expression through script writing, making costumes, finding or making props and sets, or filming a video. And indeed, some will choose to never playact again after childhood has passed. We all find our own level of comfort within the available range of dramatic expression.

Therefore, Green Light teachers do not force students to get onstage in front of others. For some students, such an experience would push them too far out of their comfort levels. Once students start operating out of fear, they are certainly not in an effective state for productive learning, and we lose the whole point of including drama as a teaching device.

Instead, we need to encourage each student to find his or her niche within the broad realm of drama. Some indeed will charge the stage with no hesitation. Others may surprise themselves by being unsure at first, and eventually discovering they love some aspect of this form of artistic endeavor. Others will find their place in a backstage or directorial role.

Drama can play a critical role in effective instruction, and teachers who utilize it wisely provide students with a lifelong gift: not just the opportunity to easily learn and remember a lesson, but also the opportunity to discover how they feel about this spectrum of self-expression. *One of the fundamental goals of the entire educational process is that students discover their personal preferences and talents along the path.* By presenting students with the wide range of expressive possibilities that come from dramatic presentation, we may put them on a path they otherwise would have failed to find.

KEY POINTS

- Writing and acting in skits helps students understand and learn.
- Props and costumes help.
- Songs can be acted out too.
- Students can actually *become* the content. (For another example of this, see Lesson 6 in the "Movement" chapter.)
- Not every student has to be an actor. Equal learning can occur when creating a script, rehearsing the crew, or directing a skit.
- Sometimes, the teacher can be the performer.
- Drama can be used for assessment as well as learning.
- Video allows content to be reviewed again and again.
- Talk shows offer wonderful assessment opportunities.
- In some cases, writing an entire play, or song, may be possible. The teacher could write the script, or the students could create it, or both could work together to develop a dramatic masterpiece!

QUESTIONS TO ASK YOURSELF

- Do you have some natural "hams" in your classroom? If so, how can you get them to help you enroll every student in becoming a part of this process?
- Do you have a space that might be used as a stage?
- Would *you* be willing to act out learning for your students?
- Where could you go to gather costumes or props?
- Are you excited about being dramatic in your classroom? If you are, chances are the students will join in your enthusiasm!

10 Visuals

Do you see what I mean?

How will you use them in <u>your</u> lessons?

ADAPT . . . ADJUST . . . APPLY

Does this happen in your classroom? Visuals are acknowledged as a critical means of communicating new information. New material is presented using graphic representations. Students create their own illustrations of the content to assist their understanding and recall, adding icons, maps, symbols, and doodles to their notes. This increased focus on visuals enhances the speed with which students grasp and remember content.

VISUALS: AN OVERVIEW

Education usually relies on *words*—oral or written—as the primary means of teaching new concepts, ideas, and information. Language, of course, can be an excellent communications tool. However, if meaning isn't reinforced by visuals, the learning process may well founder. This is because visual imagery is one of the primary ways in which human beings intake, process, and encode information.

The educational system clearly recognizes the importance of visuals, as evidenced by the fact that there are so many blackboards and whiteboards in every classroom. Unfortunately, Red Light teachers mostly use these tools to perpetuate their *verbal* communication—decorating them with words, not pictures. Green Light teachers realize that adding relevant, engaging, and practical *visuals* into their lessons can greatly enhance students' potential to understand and memorize new content.

For example, visuals that will help students understand, process, encode, and recall new information could include the following:

- Concept maps, mind maps, or other "mapping" devices
- Organizational devices for lecture notes, such as flowcharts
- A creative layout to visually organize primarily verbal information
- Graphic icons or representations of the content created by either the students or the teacher
- Cartoons on posters, in slides, or on handouts
- Symbols, figures, or sketches that illustrate a concept
- Drawings or doodles created by the students, added to their notes
- Physical "artifacts" that students not only see, but also touch, hold, and experience for themselves

This list shows just a few of the myriad of visuals that we could use in the classroom.

The *type* of visuals being used and the *frequency* with which they are used will vary according to the content. However, regardless of *how* they are included, visual support devices such as these can greatly increase the effectiveness of instruction.

We understand the power of visual communication the moment we visit a country where we don't speak the language. In this situation, we can't understand written signs or spoken language, yet we can still find our way around and understand a great deal by looking at visual cues and interpreting symbols. Think of the universal symbols for male and female bathrooms, danger, first aid, or no smoking. A simple sign says it all.

Not only do visuals communicate messages just as well as words, in some cases they actually make the point more powerfully. For example, when listening to a teacher, 55 percent of a student's comprehension comes from what they see, 38 percent comes from the tone of voice, and only 7 percent comes from the words actually spoken (Mehrabian, 1981). We may miss spoken—or written—words, yet we only need a millisecond to intake information encoded visually. Simply stated, visual information is fast and easy to take in and is highly memorable. No wonder Green Light teachers use pictures to reinforce or assist learning wherever possible.

Green Light teachers understand that symbols, diagrams, and illustrations can often communicate more effectively, accurately, and efficiently than words alone, and incorporate this powerful teaching mechanism as often as possible.

As the following lessons show, teachers have an astonishingly wide variety of ways to include more visual learning devices in the classroom. In the process, as this first demonstration illustrates, they can take a potentially dull topic and bring it vibrantly, vividly, and *visually* to life.

LESSON 1

Using novel visual teaching tools created by the teacher

Topic	Editing
Students	Fifth Grade: ages 10–11
Primary Green Light strategy	Visuals
Related strategies	Novelty, drama, movement, and emotion
Submitted by	Cindy Rickert, Fifth-Grade Teacher
	Christopher Farms Elementary School
	Virginia Beach, Virginia

Red Light. Traditionally, the curriculum calls for students to follow the writing process and edit samples of writing according to lengthy checklists. Students are given paragraphs with mistakes, and off they go . . . or at least that's the intention of the lesson. Most don't actually do it, because to them the topic seems tedious and uninteresting.

Green Light. When my students get to the editing part of the writing process, they put on white lab coats and become "Doctors of Editing." They write "prescriptions" for sick essays and paragraphs. They walk around with clipboards and "prescription pads." I created an acronym for what to look for, and we call it their "S.C.R.I.P.T." The initials stand for the six major aspects of the editing process:

- Spelling
- Capitalization
- Run-ons
- Indenting problems
- Punctuation
- Tense

Here is the visual that students use for their "prescription pad":

Pre-S.C.R.I.P.T.-ion for Writing

Dr. _____ **Edit**

Name of Writing _____

Type of Illness:	Severed spelling
	Capitalization cold
	Run-on runny nose
	Indent-itus
	Punctured punctuation
	Tense tension

Seriousness of Illness: 1   2   3   4   5

Recommended Treatment: _____

_____

_____

Now, when we get to the editing portion of the writing process, students are eager to "diagnose" and "treat" their essays. They eagerly pull out their "prescription pads" and work hard to make their writing "well." The use of the visual—the prescription pad—has taken information that was previously uninteresting to them and made it seem 10 times clearer to understand, and infinitely more interesting. The addition of clipboards and white lab coats, and the chance to play the role of a "doctor" of writing, make the visual we use even more powerful.

Effectiveness. When I used to teach this topic the traditional way, students would get to the editing portion of the writing process and skip through it. They were bored, they were distracted, and they couldn't care less. Now they *can't wait* to edit their papers!

DEBRIEF OF LESSON 1

This amazing demonstration lesson contains many Green Light strategies. Together they create a lesson that not only engages students learning the material the first time, but also provides a novel platform for subsequent skills development and review. However, for the purposes of this chapter, let us focus on the visual component of the lesson.

The key aspect of the visual used here, the "prescription pad," is how the teacher took the central information students needed to learn—the six critical components of the editing process—and presented them to her students in a clear, concise, and visibly understandable format. The "visual" that students are using becomes a lively prompt for their engagement with the content. The other Green Light strategies, such as novelty, dramatics, movement, and emotion (they *are* enjoying themselves, after all!), all flow outward from this central starting point.

Rather than relying on words alone, where possible, Green Light teachers consolidate the central concepts or key points of their lesson into a visual organization mechanism. This makes the information easier for students to grasp, allowing them to quickly learn the basics of a particular topic. Once this occurs, they are free to expend the remainder of their mental energy on understanding *how* to apply the information.

In the previous example, the *teacher* created the visual that students used to help them learn and apply the information. The other side of the equation is that sometimes *students* can create the visual apparatus they will use to encode information.

LESSON 2

Students creating visual maps of new information

Topic	AP Biology
Students	Eleventh Grade: ages 16–17
Primary Green Light strategy	Visuals
Related strategies	Novelty, memory, and socialization

Submitted by   Therese B. Vitiello, High School Science Teacher
                                North Hunterdon High School
                                Annandale, New Jersey

Red Light. This class is a rigorous, fast-paced college freshman–level biology major course taught to first-year biology students at my high school. Traditionally, lecture has been the primary means of presenting this enormous amount of material. So, that's how I originally tried to tackle the subject. Some students were able to handle the barrage of information; others weren't. Despite my best efforts, those who couldn't keep up frequently got left behind. I was frustrated and decided to look for another way to approach teaching this enormous amount of information, thinking there must be a better way—and there was!

Green Light. There's an old adage that says, "A picture is worth a thousand words." I have found that no matter how I structure my lessons, students find great success when they end each chapter by *drawing* the important ideas and condensing their thoughts onto one piece of paper. It is a perfect way for them to collect and organize the important information. I ask them to include as much color and detail and as many words—and especially pictures—as possible. I also encourage them to include some sort of logical progression to their thoughts. While these are the overall guidelines, I also explicitly encourage them to express their own individuality, personality, and style when doing their drawing. Some of the things they create are absolutely amazing!

Effectiveness. Very rapidly at the start of each year, even the most logical-mathematical students begin to tap into, unleash, and express their creativity. Students become amazed at how much information they can store and recall in picture format. Once they become familiar with this approach and experience how effective it can be in helping them learn the material we need to cover, they insist on doing this for every major piece of content. Their learning has soared, and now very few—if any—students ever get left behind.

DEBRIEF OF LESSON 2

The lesson mentions a popular adage concerning the relationship between pictures and words. Red Light teachers may counter with the saying, "The map is not the territory." While this is certainly true, a map *can* point us in the right direction, help us find our bearings, and ultimately reach our desired destination more rapidly. When driving to a place we've never been before, finding our way without a map can be quite challenging. However, with a map as a reference guide, we can choose the proper route, constantly confirm we are heading in the right direction, and reach our intended destination quickly and efficiently.

The same is true when students are learning new information, especially topics that are "content heavy." Students frequently perceive this endeavor as being similar to finding their way across vast, uncharted, unfamiliar territory. Staring at endless pages of notes they've taken during countless lectures, they can easily become devastated by the crushing weight of the sheer volume of information. Not knowing where to begin, most will stumble this way and that, veering wildly in multiple directions. Not surprisingly, they frequently become lost—frustrated in their efforts to understand the new information. When they begin to feel helpless, many will simply surrender to seemingly inevitable failure. They refuse to put forth their best effort when studying and learning, simply because they believe—sometimes quite rightly—that they'll never "get it."

A great deal of this confusion and frustration can be eliminated if we allow students to occasionally create their own "map" of new material (Goldberg, 2004). This allows them to organize their thoughts and insights into a format they can more easily understand. With this guide in hand, they can formulate a proper plan for setting out on a successful journey of discovery and learning.

The term *maps* used in the context of education has come to be known by a variety of names, such as *mind maps, concept maps, visual reference guides,* and *graphic organizers.* Regardless of the exact name, creating this type of map is a useful learning strategy that many students will use whenever they have to make sense of and learn large amounts of new material (Budd, 2004).

There are many references available to teachers interested in learning more about the theory and practice of mind maps. However, there is no single, absolute "right" way to create a useful visual map. The most important issue to consider is what is most effective for the students. Green Light teachers might consider introducing a variety of possibilities for creating a visual map and eventually allow students to choose the method that works best for them.

One of the keys to this strategy is that students are creating their *own* visual (Margulies & Valenza, 2005). When we create something of our own, it is immediately more memorable to us than someone else's work, simply because it's *ours.* We conceptualized it, designed it, and polished it, so we know it intimately. By itself, the singular idea of students using their *own* visual creations can be a powerful technique for Green Light teachers to consider, even if it is not taken as far as creating a full map of the material. This ownership aspect of visual learning is important enough to isolate and highlight on its own—and it is illustrated perfectly in this next example.

LESSON 3

Students adding graphic icons to their notes

Topic   Animal Kingdoms
Students   Fourth Grade: ages 9–10
Primary Green Light strategy   Visual
Related strategies   Socialization, novelty, and emotion
Submitted by   Jenn Currie, Fourth-Grade Teacher
                                     Commodore Perry School
                                     Hadley, Pennsylvania

Red Light. Traditionally, students would listen to a lecture on the topic of animal kingdoms, or read the text in round-robin style. Then they would complete the review questions at the end of the lesson.

Green Light. I have my students take notes using a three-column method, which I model for them. The first column is for the vocabulary word or main idea phrase. The second column is for the definition or lists of examples. The third column is for a *graphic representation of the key idea*. For example, students could draw a dog representing a mammal, a frog for a reptile, and so forth. One of the most important aspects of this instructional strategy is that students get to *choose* what they will use to represent the topic, as long as it matches the topic. Then, in their own special way, they draw it. Finally, they all turn to other students near them and compliment them on their very special drawing!

Effectiveness. Adding drawing to the lesson allows those more visually oriented students to remember the information better by using graphics to represent their learning, while everyone seems to enjoy the process! After using this method the first time for an entire unit, the test results confirmed what I expected: they remembered what they drew, and they *all* passed with a B or better!

DEBRIEF OF LESSON 3

Even in this brief lesson description, the teacher is simultaneously using multiple effective teaching strategies. One is allowing students to *choose* which animal they will draw, and letting the students draw the image, in their *own very special way,* thus giving them ownership of their creations. Having the choice of which animal to draw is important, since the idea of being allowed creative freedom can add a significant amount of power to the idea: "I made this!" Far too much of our current curriculum is created by someone else, and then "dumped" onto students to learn. Here, there is at least a semblance of balance between learning the content—animal kingdoms—and allowing students to do their own thing.

Another important aspect of this lesson is encouraging the students to share their creation with other students. This social process, which also includes their receiving acknowledgment for their efforts, keeps students engaged and serves to further cement the memory in place.

Yet another important aspect is relating the image they are drawing directly to the content, which can help spark later memories. However, while it is useful and effective in this particular circumstance, it is important to clarify that the visuals students create do not always have to be specifically related to the content they are learning, as shown in Bonus Idea 2 at the end of this chapter.

Note also how the teacher *intentionally directs the students to make space on their paper for their drawings*. Some students may be hesitant to draw anything on a page where they've taken notes, since it goes against their previous instructions from Red Light teachers. In Red Light classrooms, teachers actively discourage students—especially older students—from adding images to pages with their notes, insisting that drawing is childish. In fact, as we get older and material becomes more complex, creating personal visuals to make sense of material and prompt its recall becomes even more important.

To overcome students' apprehension about creating their own visuals, Green Light teachers may well need to deliberately instruct students where to add images, allocate time during the lesson specifically for student drawing, and conspicuously encourage them in their efforts (Pineda De Romero & Dwyer, 2005).

Thus, Green Light teachers actively wage war against the current trend of repressing students' freedom to use their own images and drawings when taking notes. When their creatively is unleashed, the energy it releases can be pointed in the proper direction, as shown in the next lesson.

LESSON 4

Using visuals to assess learning and understanding

Topic	Second Language Literacy
Students	Second–Fifth Grades: ages 7–11
Primary Green Light strategy	Visual
Related strategies	Movement, socialization, and memory
Submitted by	Karoline Gebbett, Foreign Language Teacher
	Mountbatten Languages College
	Southampton, England

Red Light. Reading in second languages is traditionally taught from a textbook with pictures. Students are asked to translate a sentence, or answer true or false.

Green Light. We play a type of Pictionary game. Students are given 15 sentences on a piece of paper. One student picks a sentence from a box and has to *draw* a visual representation of the sentence on the board. Students then race to guess which sentence, from the 15 on their sheet, is being drawn. For homework, I ask them to draw a picture to represent each of the sentences.

Effectiveness. I find this lesson connects with all my students. The kids who get turned off when we open a book are motivated to translate the sentences because they want to win the game, and they enjoy drawing in general. The whole class is completely engaged and I have no discipline problems. The students also engage well with the homework: drawing pictures is so much more appealing than translating sentences, yet it tests the same competency.

DEBRIEF OF LESSON 4

This lesson introduces an entirely different angle on the use of visuals—*assessment of understanding* (Fernandes, Rodriques, & Lindsey, 2005). Much of learning a new language, at least in the initial stages, is verbal. However, foreign language teachers often face the challenge of avoiding the "parroting" effect. This occurs when students verbally repeat a word, phrase, or sentence—but really have no idea what they are saying. The use of visuals offers teachers a unique way of checking for understanding, while doing the necessary review. Not only is repeated practice vital, but *varying* the way it is done is equally important.

In fact, this idea of varying the review format is important in learning almost any new information. This is because multiple ways of *reviewing* content offer multiple ways of *remembering* it. Straightforward repetition can rapidly become boring, making students tune out. By instead allowing them to participate in a game, which involves movement, social interaction, and creating pictures, the students remain attentive while developing *corresponding corridors of cognition*.

Using visuals as a means of assessing learning can work several ways. For example, the teacher could provide a sentence and students could draw a related picture or the teacher could provide a picture and students could create a relevant sentence describing it. Or students could have one set of cards with pictures and another set of cards with sentences written on them. Individually or in small groups, they could attempt to match the picture with the correct sentence. In each of these cases, the teacher will be able to assess students' comprehension.

The following lesson expands on this concept, but with a novel twist of its own.

LESSON 5

Teaching a concept through the use of a graphic opposite

Topic	Geometry Terms
Students	Fourth Grade: ages 9–10
Primary Green Light strategy	Visual
Related strategies	Emotion, socialization, and novelty
Submitted by	Jenn Currie, Fourth-Grade Teacher
	Commodore Perry School
	Hadley, Pennsylvania

Red Light. Traditionally, students are introduced to geometry terms by reading definitions in the textbook. They practice using the example in the textbook and are quizzed two or three days later.

Green Light. In my class, I give students "is/isn't" cards. These cards are blank, except for four empty boxes labeled "Word," "Definition," "Graphic," and "NOT!" Students are introduced to no more than five relevant terms. Either as individuals or as a small group, they look up the definitions in the glossary or off of our "math word wall." Discussion determines what that term may *look* like, and as a class we draw a graphic representation of that term in the first box; for instance, they would draw an example of perpendicular lines. In the box beside it, we draw what it is "not."

Students are encouraged to draw a picture that is similar to the given term, but different in some important way, so they learn these are *not* the same things. For example, they could draw a picture of lines that are not perpendicular, intersecting at an angle other than 90 degrees. These cards are kept in the classroom, and randomly they are pulled out and practiced with a partner.

Effectiveness. This way of teaching geometry terms has been very effective because the students define and draw each term, and because they love to creatively draw something in the "not" box! The percentage of students recalling the meaning of terms has risen dramatically. Even if they aren't capable of defining the word, they are capable of showing a visual representation of what a term is and isn't. That shows me they understand, and eventually leads to their becoming comfortable with that term.

DEBRIEF OF LESSON 5

Teaching mathematics often lends itself quite naturally to the use of visuals. For example, geometry would be incredibly difficult—if not impossible—to understand without pictures and drawings of points, lines, angles, and circles. So using visuals to teach this subject seems automatic. However, this teacher is handling the visual aspect of the learning process in a novel way—she has added a unique twist that can be applicable when teaching a wide range of subjects.

The crucial added component is the use of the "not" image. By drawing something that is similar, but not quite right, students are learning to make finer and finer points of distinction about the terms. Often the assumption is that if they know what something *is*, then they must automatically know what it is *not*, and this is *not* always the case. Teachers from all content areas could look at their subject matter and determine where they could visually use the idea of "close, but not quite" when teaching.

For example, suppose middle school history students are studying what uniforms soldiers from different countries wore during World War II. To explain this, a Red Light teacher would simply show pictures of one country's uniforms, then show another and then another. The Green Light teacher might begin by simultaneously showing students pictures of soldiers' uniforms from *different countries* and asking them to compare and contrast the uniforms for differences and similarities.

Next, they might be shown pictures of soldiers from the *same* country wearing uniforms from different eras. The design of the uniforms would be much more similar than in the first round, although there would certainly be differences. Again, students could point out and articulate these distinctions. Perhaps the next layer of complexity would be showing them pictures where something about the uniform is incorrect, and they are asked to identify what is not right about it. The smaller the difference is between the actual concept begin taught and the "not" version, the clearer the students' understanding of what is correct.

Using images or pictures that help students more clearly understand important concepts is central to effectively incorporating visuals in teaching. This next lesson makes this point in a BIG way!

LESSON 6

Combining multiple visuals into a single large image

Topic	Plot Structure
Students	Fifth Grade: ages 10–11
Primary Green Light strategy	Visuals
Related strategies	Socialization, connections, novelty, and memory
Submitted by	Cindy Rickert, Fifth-Grade Teacher
	Christopher Farms Elementary School
	Virginia Beach, Virginia

Red Light. Traditionally, the curriculum calls for the students to read a story then plot the problem, rising action, climax, and resolution on a worksheet. The teacher lectures on what each part of the plot structure means. A multiple-choice test is given, asking them to identify the elements of plot structure.

Green Light. After we read a story, together we write a sequence of events. Then students form small groups and draw the scenes on huge whiteboards. One team lies on the ground, holding their story scene up. The next team holds their whiteboard a bit higher. Each team holds their visual progressively higher until the team with the climax scene is on their tiptoes or on a chair. The next team holds up their illustrations slightly below the climax, and so on until the resolution is complete. This both visually and physically shows students how stories progress, and how the plot structure is like a roller coaster. Now when we read a story, the students ask eagerly, "Can we make a roller coaster today with the whiteboards?" Excited inquiries of this kind are a teacher's dream.

Effectiveness. When I originally taught this topic, I would write the objectives on the board and inform the students, "Today we are learning about plot structure." Immediately, they would shut down. I don't blame them, since "plot structure" sounds so boring! Now, I just have them tell "roller coaster stories" and have them draw pictures. While still learning about plot structure, they no longer have that negative attitude. They engage in the lesson quickly and easily, and learn rapidly. Needless to say, *reading scores are through the roof*. Most importantly, my students are excited to read a new story every week.

DEBRIEF OF LESSON 6

Visuals obviously form the core of this instructional strategy. However, there are some notable distinctions in how they are being used here as compared with previous demonstration lessons:

- first, they are being created by a *group* of students;
- second, they are much *larger* than a single piece of paper; and
- third, they are *physically combined* to create a *very* large overall image of the content students are learning.

In particular, lining up the posters across the classroom to create a dramatic visual image of the key content is a powerful idea for ending the lesson, cementing the central concept in the students' minds (Baghban, 2007).

One of the central tenets of the Green Light teaching philosophy is trying hundreds of different ways to help students learn. The following Bonus Idea demonstrates this in a singularly brilliant fashion, showing how teachers who think beyond Red Light boundaries can create amazing results.

BONUS IDEA 1: THE CLASSROOM AS A MUSEUM

Using three-dimensional visual artifacts to teach all subjects

Topics   History, social studies, English, and more
Students   All grades, all ages
Primary Green Light strategy   Visuals
Related Strategies   Novelty, drama, connections, and more
Submitted by   Keil Hileman, Eighth-Grade Teacher
                              Monticello Trails Middle School
                              Shawnee, Kansas

Red Light. In general, education is traditionally done with very few pictures, a great deal of writing, note taking, and limited discussions. Yet the world we live in is very much a *visual* learning environment. The reliance on limited textbooks, with limited visual stimulation and almost no hands-on connections, continues to foster a very limited learning curve for our students.

Green Light. There are many different ways Green Light teachers can use what I call the "museum artifacts" approach in their teaching.* My definition for an artifact is *any object used to teach a lesson.* The following is just a brief list of some of the many techniques I use every day to educate and motivate my students:

Beginnings. I present an artifact they have not seen before and we guess about what it might be, how it was used, and why it is significant to the topic of discussion. It is a great way to introduce a unit and assess students' prior knowledge.

Research Topics. I take a carefully chosen item, give my students a few clues about it, and send them on a research-gathering adventure. I call this the "Mystery in History" activity.

Touch Tables. I take all of the artifacts connected to the current unit and keep them out on a table while the unit is being taught. Students are free to read about them, touch them, and study them.

Storytelling: Written and Oral Projects. I have students either choose an artifact or I assign one to them randomly. They create a story about it using the vocabulary or concepts from the current unit. Ultimately, the story can be oral or written, real or fictional—they all work!

---

*Keil Hileman earned the distinction of being Kansas Teacher of the Year in 2004 and is a nationally recognized speaker. For further information on his innovative "Turning the Classroom Into a Museum" ideas, he can be reached at keilh@usd232.org.

Drama Props. Plays and dramatizations can be a great way to utilize artifacts. We did a short Greek play one year, using Roman and Middle Ages replica swords for the guards and king. While they were not historically accurate, the students had a blast and could explain to anyone why the swords were not really Greek in design.

Cultural Examples. I'm always collecting artifacts that can be used as a source of information about various cultures and their defining values. The most common question my students seem to have about other cultures is, "Why do they do that?" Analyzing and studying a related artifact or two from that culture often helps answer those types of questions.

Memory Triggers. Simply being surrounded by all of these visual artifacts, students are continually surrounded by history and what they are studying. They will often look around the room during tests and see an artifact that will "trigger" a memory and help them with the test. I also answer questions during the exams by reminding them to go look at a key artifact. I love to see their eyes light up as they shoot me that secret smile that says, "Now I remember!"

Random Vocabulary Review. I take an artifact that has a connection to the unit I am teaching and have students describe it. Sometimes they do this as one long story. Each student must use at least one vocabulary word from the unit in their sentence. When I do this orally, I have the whole class stand in a circle and hold their notes. After the first student has created a sentence, they sit down and choose the next person to speak.

Assessment. I take all of the artifacts that have been included during the teaching of a unit and use them in the exam. This can be done using a myriad of oral or written methods. I prefer to just list them and have the students define them from memory and in their own words. It always amazes me which parts of the artifact's story students remember.

Effectiveness. My students look forward to being in my class each day. They never know what new items they will see and learn about. This sense of anticipation and excitement is invaluable as an instructional tool. Students work hard to get to my room on time. They are motivated to complete their homework, quizzes, and exams to reach project times, show-and-tell sessions, or "pass-around" days. What makes all this magic happen? Just by having the artifacts readily available in the classroom, students want to touch, examine, and explore—it prompts everything we do!

DEBRIEF OF BONUS IDEA 1

Given the success this innovative teacher is experiencing, all teachers might want to consider how any artifacts could be used to teach any subject. By turning his classroom in a museum, this teacher has created an innovative, unique, and visually stimulating learning environment.

BONUS IDEA 2: THE ART OF
THE *DELIBERATE* DOODLE

Creating a freedom of expression for the use of visuals in all subject areas

Topics	Anything and everything
Students	All grades, all ages
Primary Green Light strategy	Visuals
Related Strategies	Memory, novelty, socialization, and emotion
Submitted by	Wayne Logue, Professional Cartoonist
	Education Illustrated, LLC
	Auckland, New Zealand

Red Light. The teacher talks and students take notes.

Green Light. Has the following situation ever happened? You are in a classroom, listening well, concentrating intently, and furiously taking notes. At one point, you get distracted and end up doodling off to the side of page 8. Eventually, you catch yourself and refocus your attention back on the lecture. Later, in preparation for the quiz, you carefully review those notes. You go to take the test, and . . . what's the *first* thing you can remember, the thing that sticks out most in your mind? It's that darn doodle from page 8!

If something like that has ever happened to you, the important question to ask is, "Why do I remember that image so well?" Try this brief experiment:

Right now, keep you eyes focused on this page, and think of any object in the room around you where you are reading right now. Think of another one, and now another one. Stop. Now read on . . .

When you tried that experiment, what jumped into your mind first, the *image* of each object or the *word* that describes the object? For almost everyone, the *image* will appear first in our minds. This is because our brains tend to naturally create visual images. In fact, at some level, we actually *think* in pictures.

Green Light teachers can take advantage of this instinctive mental reaction. Rather than having a meaningless, random doodle appear in the students' minds, adjust the basic idea and use it to *deliberately help students remember key information*. Instead of

1

Start by drawing an "f" shape at the front, and connect the cross-stroke to the "r." Now draw the under curves and you have made the eyes.

2

Give him some eyeballs then make a curve from the tip of the "f" hook to the top of the "g" downstroke. Fill in the "o" and "g" and add a few extra spots.

frog

3

Using the bottom of the first eye and the curve of the "r" as a guide, draw his mouth. Now draw a curve over the "g" loop and continue along to make his back foot.

4

All you need to do now is add his front foot and a small line to show his belly, and he is ready to hop!

frog

EDUCATION Illustrated

1

Draw a "t" at the front and then close the "c" to make it into a circle.

2

Going straight up from the top of the "t"s, make triangles into the top of the head and add some other lines to the "t"s for the whiskers.

cat

3

Give him eyes, a nose, and a mouth. Add lines to the "a" and fill it in to make him a tom with a patch.

4

Draw a "w" shape on its side at the bottom of the two "t"s. Then just join the "w"s to make his jaw.

cat

EDUCATION Illustrated

1

Draw a circle above the "o" and "g." This is the first eye.

2

Draw a line from the top of the "o" and loop it up to the top of the "d" to form the top of the head and ear.

3

Fill in the "g," leaving a small circle. This is the highlight on the nose. Now just add a dot on the "o" and the other circle you drew so he can see you.

4

Finish him with a mouth, neck lines, and collar.

1

Start with a nice big curve from the top of the first "b" to the second "b" and then over and around the "y." You will have the baby"s head and bottom done.

2

Next, draw a line connecting the baby"s bottom curve and the bottom of the "y." Now draw the line from the bottom of the "b" to make the front hand.

3

Make a small curve on the back side of the first "b" and then continue it under to connect the bottom of the "b"s to make the jaw.

4

Only a few details are left: the nose, mouth, eyes, ears, and a little twirl of hair.

accidentally thinking of a meaningless doodle, teachers could ask their students to deliberately doodle on their notes. If students add arrows connecting the doodle or drawing to a key fact on that page of notes, when they recall it, the memory of the visual will act as a trigger for the memory of the key idea.

When encouraging students to deliberately create doodles on the same pages as their notes, the biggest resistance will usually be, "But I can't draw!" If the goal of the doodling process was to create a museum-quality masterpiece, in most cases this assessment would be quite right. However, that's *not* the objective here—any attempt at a visual will work quite effectively, whether it is a stick figure, a vague sketch, or an unusual or weird design—*anything*.

Despite this, most people still need a little encouragement to push them into a willingness to "draw" (Heath & Wolf, 2005). The "WordToons"* on pages 165 and 166 can help even the least creative students to draw something satisfyingly recognizable. The idea is to start with a simple word and, by adding a few lines, create something that looks like the object the word describes. Give it a try right now.

Effectiveness. It's often surprising how even just a little success in this area can inspire people to be more adventurous with the visual process. Consider teaching your students how to draw simple images such as these, and then encourage them to gradually expand their visual horizons. Once they become more comfortable drawing and doodling, invite them to add doodles, figures, or other colorful images to their notes that connect in some manner to the information they are learning.

DEBRIEF OF BONUS IDEA 2

For students who are naturally visually oriented—and often many who don't at first believe they are visually oriented—this freedom to doodle can be critical to their success in the classroom. It can create a sense of autonomy, self-sufficiency, and independence (Edwards, 1989). The lack of *any* restrictions often opens up students' minds to a multitude of possibilities for taking notes, studying, and learning. The opportunity to draw, sketch, or in any way add illustrations to their notes can become one of the most effective recall techniques they will encounter during their educational career.

KEY POINTS

- Visual imagery is one of the primary ways we naturally intake, process, and encode information.
- The *type* and *frequency* of the visuals being used to teach can vary greatly.

*For further information on Wayne Logue's book of WordToons or any of his other current creative endeavors, visit the educationillustrated.com Web site.

- Verbal material can often be presented in a concise visual format, making it easier for students to conceptually organize the key aspects of the new content.
- *Maps* help students process and recall information.
- Teachers may need to deliberately instruct students to add images to their notes and provide classroom time for this endeavor.
- Visuals can be used to *assess* student understanding.
- Drawing an *opposite visual* can also serve as a comprehension check, since before creating an *opposite*, they must understand the *original*.
- Large visuals add the element of novelty.
- *Artifacts* can teach almost any topic and bring it vividly to life for students.
- *Deliberate doodles* help students recall key information.

QUESTIONS TO ASK YOURSELF

- How often do you currently use visuals when teaching? Are there ways you can add more, especially with material that is essentially verbal?
- What sections do your students currently struggle with? Can you add some type of visual especially in these places that might help them learn better?
- What kind of artifacts, if any, would match your topic and help students learn? Where can you go to begin gathering these items?
- Are there talented artists among your students? If so, how can you make use of their talents so all students benefit? Could they draw on the chalkboard, or create drawings that can be copied and shared with everyone?
- How comfortable are you with allowing students to creatively doodle? Remember, they follow your lead—are you willing to not only allow, but *encourage* this visually creative behavior?

Final Note

Having read through this book, you may be feeling slightly overwhelmed at the thought of figuring out how to best utilize so many wonderful ideas. If so, relax! Yes, it can be a huge step to change even a few of our ingrained professional habits. Yet, as the contributing teachers in this book would surely tell you, it takes time—as well as courage—to bring these Green Light teaching strategies fully to life in your classroom. My advice to educators willing to move more into Green Light teaching is simply this:

> *Start small.* You don't have to apply every strategy at once. Pick the ones you feel most comfortable with, and take a small step forward into the Green Light zone. Evaluate the success of that strategy, adjust and adapt it until it starts to become a natural part of your planning process and an integral part of your teaching style. When using this strategy starts to feel easy and natural, select another one and repeat the process.

Whatever shade of Green you introduce in your classroom, just remember that the fundamental theme of Green Light teaching is to

teach the <u>students</u>, NOT the <u>content</u>.

If you do this—if you adapt teaching strategies to the needs of your students—you will make an astonishing difference in their learning and, ultimately, in their lives.

Appendix

The Rock Cycle Play

By Emma Jeter, Christopher Farms Elementary,
Virginia Beach, Virginia

THE GREATEST ROCK OF ALL

Narrator 1:	A mighty group of rocks was perched high upon a mountaintop. This particular rock formed part of the peak of the magnificent mountain.
Rock 1:	We are the highest and mightiest rocks of all.
Rock 2:	No rocks are higher and mightier than us.
Narrator 1:	But the wind blew strong on that mountaintop.
Wind:	Whoosh, whoosh! I will blow you all to bits.
Rock 3:	We are the mightiest rocks of all—you will not break us!
Rain:	I am cold, cold rain, and I will fall hard upon you with traces of acid to break you down.
Rock 2:	No rocks are higher and mightier than us—you will not break us!
Narrator 2:	The wind and cold acid rain fell upon the rocks, but the rocks were strong and withstood the weathering for a long time. But gradually the rocks began to weaken.
Rock 3:	Oh no, oh no, I am breaking apart. I am breaking into tiny pieces.

Wind:	That's right! You have been weathered into sediments and will be washed away!
Rock 1:	Oh no!!
Stream:	I am a stream and you must come with me.
Narrator 2:	The stream soon became a river as it rushed down the mighty mountain, taking all the sediments with it.
Sediment 1:	We have been rushing down river for hundreds, maybe thousands, of years.
Sediment 2:	I know. I for one am tired of being a single sediment. But what can we do?
Sediment 3:	I have an idea, but it means that we have to pile ourselves on top of other sediments.
Sediment 2:	How will that help? It sounds a bit weird to me.
Sediment 3:	If we pile on top of lots of other sediments in layers, the weight of all the layers will stop us rushing downstream forever.
Sediment 1:	Well, it sounds strange, but I'm willing to try anything at this point.
Narrator 3:	So the sediments piled on top of each other and on top of other sediments that had been deposited by the river. The weight of the layers above compacted the sediments together until a new kind of rock was formed.
Narrator 4:	What was the name of this new kind of rock?
All Rocks:	(shouting) SEDIMENTARY ROCK!
Rock 4:	I am the most beautiful rock in the world. Nothing can break me.
Rock 5:	I have beautiful layers and I am protected by water.
Rock 6:	I am underwater, where wind and rain cannot weather me.
Narrator 4:	But as the rock was compacted and pushed further and further underground, he noticed something a little uncomfortable.
Rock 4:	Oh no, oh no!
Rock 5:	What's wrong?
Rock 6:	It's getting hotter and hotter. The pressure is too much.
Rock 5:	Get a grip, will you? We are the most beautiful kind of rock. Nothing can happen to us.

Narrator 5:	But as we all know, pride comes before a fall. Before he knew what was happening, the sedimentary rock was deep inside the earth.
Rock 7:	I feel different. It's hot and the pressure here is immense.
Rock 8:	I know what you mean. I am being changed by chemicals.
Rock 9:	I am morphing into something different.
Rock 10:	Me too. I am changing and morphing.
Narrator 6:	How the rock wished that he was back on the crust of the earth where the cool wind blew. But now he was changed. What had he become?
All Rocks:	(shouting) METAMORPHIC ROCK!
Rock 7:	I am the most beautiful rock of all. I have gone through so much in my little rock life.
Rock 8:	I know—I used to be the mightiest rock of all, then I was the most beautiful sedimentary rock. Then I was morphed through heat, pressure, and chemicals into metamorphic rock. Nothing can touch me now. I am the best rock in the world.
Narrator 7:	But as the rock was talking, they began to notice something else.
Rock 9:	Wow! It's hotter than it was last summer.
Rock 10:	Are you complaining again? You're always complaining! You are never happy.
Rock 9:	I would be happy, but I think I'm melting. So are you!
Rock 10:	Oh my gosh, you are right. What is happening? Why can't things ever stay the same?
Narrator 7:	The rock was now deeper into the earth and was no longer a solid rock. How the rock wished to be back on the crust where the cool wind blew.
Rock 11:	I like being magma. I'm beautiful orange and I boil slowly, deep within the earth's surface. I never have to cool down.
Rock 12:	Yeah! We like it hot. Hot, hot, hot.
Narrator 8:	Suddenly the magma felt itself being squeezed slowly toward the surface.

Rock 11:	Oh no, there is a gap in the earth's crust. We are going to be pushed through it. Help!
Narrator 9:	Some of the magma burst through the crust and down the side of a volcano. It cooled and hardened as the cool wind blew into black, glassy volcanic rocks.
Rock 12:	I am the shiniest rock of all.
Rock 13:	I am the highest and mightiest rock of all.
Rock 14:	No rocks are higher and mightier than us.
Narrator 10:	But the wind blew strong on that mountaintop and we all know what happens to rocks when the wind blows . . .

(All students now sing . . .)

The Rock Cycle Rock

Oh oh oh oh oh, ROCK CYCLE,   Oh oh oh oh oh, ROCK CYCLE,
Oh oh oh oh oh, ROCK CYCLE,   Oh oh oh oh oh, ROCK CYCLE

From a volcano shoots igneous rock,
Molten lava cools as hard as a rock,

Shiny and glassy as it hardens on the ground,

It's gonna put you in a trance when we sing it loud!

Cause you gotta know . . .

Rock cycle! Rock cycle! Rock cycle!

WE ROCK!

Oh oh oh oh oh, ROCK CYCLE,   Oh oh oh oh oh, ROCK CYCLE

Weathered and eroded it breaks into bits,

Washed away in rivers when the ground it hits,

Packs into layers at the bottom of the creek,

Sedimentary rock is what we seek.

And you know the

Rock cycle! Rock cycle! Rock cycle!

Rocking round enough?

Rock cycle! Rock cycle! Rock cycle!

WE ROCK!

Oh oh oh oh oh, ROCK CYCLE,   Oh oh oh oh oh, ROCK CYCLE,
Oh oh oh oh oh, ROCK CYCLE,   Oh oh oh oh oh, ROCK CYCLE

Pushed under ground with pressure and heat,

Transformed into rock called metamorphic,

That means change,

That means change,

That means change,

Metamorphic!

Rock cycle! Rock cycle! Rock cycle!

WE ROCK!

Oh oh oh oh oh, ROCK CYCLE,   Oh oh oh oh oh, ROCK CYCLE,
Oh oh oh oh oh, ROCK CYCLE,   Oh oh oh oh oh, ROCK CYCLE

References

Alna, O. (1999). Importance of oral storytelling in literacy development. *Ohio Reading Teacher, 33*(1), 15–18.

Baghban, M. (2007). Scribbles, labels, and stories: The role of drawing in the development of writing. *Young Children, 62*(1), 20–26.

Baumgarten, S. (2006). Meaningful movement for children: Stay true to their natures. *Teaching Elementary Physical Education*, July, 9–11.

Brand, S. T. (2006). Facilitating emergent literacy skills: A literature-based, multiple intelligence approach. *Journal of Research in Childhood Education, 21*(2), 133–148.

Budd, J. W. (2004). Mind maps as classroom exercises. *Journal of Economic Education, 35*(1), 35–46.

Chapman, M. (2007). Theory and practice of teaching discourse intonation. *ELT Journal, 61*(1), 3–11.

Cropley, A. (2006). Dimensions of creativity, creativity: A social approach. *Roeper Review, 28*(3), 125–130.

Cruz, B. C., & Murthy, S. A. (2006). Breathing life into history: Using role-playing to engage students. *Social Studies and the Young Learner, 19*(1), 4–8.

Edwards, B. (1989). *Drawing on the right side of the brain: A course in enhancing creativity and artistic confidence.* Los Angeles: Jeremy P. Tarcher.

Fernandes, P., Rodriques, S., & Lindsey, G. (2005). Critical analysis on the use of poster display as an alternative evaluation method in basic biochemistry. *Biochemistry and Molecular Biology Education, 33*(4), 281–283.

Fernandez-Berrocaal, P., & Santamaria, C. (2006). Mental models in social interaction. *The Journal of Experimental Education, 74*(3), 229–248.

Goldberg, C. (2004). Brain friendly techniques: Mind mapping. *School Library Media Activities Monthly, 21*(3), 22–24.

Green, J. (2002). *The Green book of songs by subject: The thematic guide* (5th ed.). Nashville, TN: Professional Desk References, www.greenbooksofsongs.com.

Hannaford, C. (2005). *Smart moves.* Salt Lake City, UT: Great River Books.

Hanze, M., & Berger, R. (2007). Cooperative learning, motivational effects, and student characteristics: An experimental study comparing cooperative learning and direct instruction in 12th grade physics classes. *Learning and Instruction, 17*(1), 29–41.

Heath, S. B., & Wolf, S. (2005). Focus in creative learning: Drawing on art for language development. *Literacy, 39*(1), 38–45.

Heywood, B. G. (2004). Using chants to teach almost anything! *Teaching Music, 12*(3), 48.

Jensen, E. (2002). *Learning with the body in mind*. Thousand Oaks, CA: Corwin Press.

Jensen, E. (2005). *Teaching with the brain in mind* (2nd ed.). Alexandria, VA: ASCD.

Lin, H., Chen, T., & Dwyer, F. (2006). Effects of static visuals and computer-generated animations in facilitating immediate and delayed achievement in the EFL classroom. *Foreign Language Annals, 39*(2), 203–219.

Margulies, N., & Valenza, C. (2005). *Visual thinking: Tools for mapping your ideas*. Carmarthen, UK: Crown House.

Mehrabian, A. (1981). *Silent messages: A primer of non-verbal communication*. Belmont, CA: Wadsworth.

Mercer, N., & Sams, C. (2006). Teaching children how to use language to solve math problems. *Language and Education, 20*(6), 507–528.

Miller, J., & Schwanenflugel, P. J. (2006). Prosody of syntactically complex sentences in the oral reading of young children. *Journal of Educational Psychology, 98*(4), 839–853.

Moore, J. R. (2007). Popular music helps students focus on important social issues. *Middle School Journal, 38*(4), 221–229.

Moreno, R., & Mayer, R. E. (2000). Engaging students in active learning: The case for personalized multimedia messages. *Journal of Educational Psychology, 92*(4), 724–733.

Moura, H. (2006). Analyzing multimodal interaction within a classroom setting. *Visible Language, 40*(3), 270–291.

Myhill, D., Jones, S., & Hopper, R. (2005). *Talking, listening, and learning*. Maidenhead, UK: Open University Press, 2005.

Paulin, M. G. (2005). Evolutionary origins and principles of distributed neural computation for state estimation and movement control in vertebrates. *Complexity, 10*(3), 56–65.

Pica, R. (2006). Learning in leaps and bounds. *Teaching Elementary Physical Education, 17*(3), 31–34.

Pierce, J., & Terry, K. (2000). Breathe life into history through story in the elementary classroom. *Southern Social Studies Journal, 25*(2), 77–90.

Pineda De Romero, L., & Dwyer, F. (2005). The effect of varied rehearsal strategies used to complement visualized instruction in facilitating achievement of different learning objectives. *International Journal of Instructional Media, 32*(3), 259.

Pontefract, C., & Hardman, F. (2005). The discourse of classroom interaction in Kenyan primary schools. *Comparative Education, 41*(1), 87–106.

Prensky, M. (2005). Engage me or enrage me: What today's learners demand. *Educause Review, 40*(5), 60–64.

Qais, F. (2007). Enlightening advantages of cooperative learning. ERIC online submission.

Reid, L. (2000). Professional links: Active and interactive approaches to poetry, drama and classics. *English Journal*, May, 151–155.

Robinson, K. (2001). *Out of our minds: Learning to be creative*. Oxford, UK: Capstone.

Ruhl, K., Hughes, C., & Schloss, P. (1987). Using the pause procedure to enhance lecture recall. *Teacher Education and Special Education, 10*(1), 14–18.

Schiefele, U. (1991). Interest, learning, and motivation. *Educational Psychologist, 26*(3–4), 299–323.

Sousa, D. A. (2002). *How the gifted brain learns*. Thousand Oaks, CA: Corwin Press.

Summerford, C. (2000). *PE for me*. Champaign, IL: Human Kinetics.

Sutton, J. (1998). Setting the stage: Creative drama in the writing classroom. *Stage of the Art, 9*(7), 11–15.

Tate, M. (2002). *Worksheets don't grow dendrites*. Thousand Oaks, CA: Corwin Press.

Wells, G., & Arauz, R. M. (2006). Dialogue in the classroom. *Journal of the Learning Sciences, 15*(3), 379–428.

Williams, R. B. (2007). *Cooperative learning: A standard for high achievement*. Thousand Oaks, CA: Corwin Press.

Willis, J. (2005). Adding the science of learning to the art of teaching. *Voices From the Middle, 13*(2), 30–34.

Wilson, S. (2004). Creative projects stimulate classroom learning. *Science Scope,* October, 41–43.

Wolfolk, A. (2004). *Educational psychology* (7th ed.). Boston: Allyn & Bacon.

Zachopoulou, E., Trevlas, E., & Konstadinidou, E. (2006). The design and implementation of a physical education program to promote children's creativity in the early years. *International Journal of Early Years Education, 14*(3), 279–294.

Index

CORWIN PRESS

The Corwin Press logo—a raven striding across an open book—represents the union of courage and learning. Corwin Press is committed to improving education for all learners by publishing books and other professional development resources for those serving the field of PreK–12 education. By providing practical, hands-on materials, Corwin Press continues to carry out the promise of its motto: **"Helping Educators Do Their Work Better."**